Manna
for Today
Bread from heaven for each day

SINDY NAGEL

WestBow
PRESS
A DIVISION OF THOMAS NELSON

Scriptures taken from the Holy Bible, New International Version®, NIV®. Copyright © 1973, 1978, 1984, 2011 by Biblica, Inc.™ Used by permission of Zondervan. All rights reserved worldwide. www.zondervan.com. The "NIV" and "New International Version" are trademarks registered in the United States Patent and Trademark Office by Biblica, Inc.™

WestBow Press books may be ordered through booksellers or by contacting:

WestBow Press
A Division of Thomas Nelson
1663 Liberty Drive
Bloomington, IN 47403
www.westbowpress.com
1-(866) 928-1240

Because of the dynamic nature of the Internet, any web addresses or links contained in this book may have changed since publication and may no longer be valid. The views expressed in this work are solely those of the author and do not necessarily reflect the views of the publisher, and the publisher hereby disclaims any responsibility for them.

Any people depicted in stock imagery provided by Shutterstock are models, and such images are being used for illustrative purposes only.
Certain stock imagery © Shutterstock

ISBN: 978-1-4497-6704-4 (sc)
ISBN: 978-1-4497-6705-1 (hc)
ISBN: 978-1-4497-6703-7 (e)

Library of Congress Control Number: 2012917050

Printed in the United States of America

WestBow Press rev. date: 10/19/2012

"Sindy Nagel is an excellent communicator on explaining The Father's heart and love toward us, His children. Taking the scriptures and breaking them down into The Father's perspective make them come alive in a new and fresh way. I highly recommend you get this book, and add it to your daily devotional reading. It truly is *Manna for Today!*"
— Beth Jones, Author of *Getting A Grip On The Basics Series*

"Intimacy with Jesus is the quest of every serious Christ-follower…but who's chasing who? Sindy's devotional reveals the heart of God, a God who pursues and captures the hearts of His own. Read it, and grow."
— Dr. Jeff Porte, Centerpoint Church, Kalamazoo, Michigan

"I have read *Manna for Today* devotional book, and find it highly inspirational for all Christians." — Harold Ferris, Michigan State University Alumni

"In these pages, we meet with a God who loves us infinitely. *Manna for Today* gives hope as God speaks through the author. I look forward to reading this each day, and enjoy the Bible verses related to each devotional." – Julie, a long-time friend

"I felt like God spoke to me personally through these devotionals, exactly when I needed it most." — A woman of the faith

"I highly recommend Sindy's devotional, *Manna for Today*. It directs your focus, first and foremost, to God's Holy Word at the beginning of each page, and she intricately weaves His Scripture throughout her inspirations. They are light in a world with much darkness. Let her devotionals help light His path for you!" — Paula, a wife, mother, and registered nurse

"*Manna for Today* is a daily reminder that I am a child of God, loved by God, and protected by God. It is spiritual nourishment at its best! What a way to start your day—with a daily transfusion that restores your soul and instantly lifts you up." — Sally, a sister in Christ

"I love seeing the Scripture printed first, and then reading the devotional words for the day. The discipline of quieting myself each day with this book has enhanced my 'alone time' with the Lord!"
— Sue, a mom in Idaho

"Sindy is a godly woman, gentle, and kind. Her devotional takes God's word, and gives you a practical lesson to apply to your everyday life. You will be blessed by reading her inspirational messages." —Sandra, a wife and mother of three in Michigan

This book is dedicated to
Jesus Christ, my heavenly husband,
who laid down his life for me, his bride,
and to Doug, my earthly husband,
who laid down his life for me, putting
my desires before his own, to afford me
the time and resources to be used
by God in this endeavor.
I love you both with all my heart!

Contents

TABLE OF CONTENTS

Note: The first two devotionals in the "Glorify Me" chapter are written in the voice of God, while the remaining devotionals in the chapter are written in the voice of the author/reader, in order to give God the honor and glory that he desires and deserves.

Preface

My passion for sharing the whispers of the Holy Spirit is the driving force behind the writing of this book. My name is on the front of this book, but I do not claim to be the author of it, nor do I take any credit for its content. I was simply the pen God held in his hand as he created this work. This book is solely the inspired work of God, as given to me through the voice of his Holy Spirit, and the reading of his Holy Scripture. It is my earnest prayer that the words on these pages will bring you blessing, comfort, and encouragement as you feel the love of God poured out to you through the voice of each member of the Trinity: Father, Son, and Holy Spirit.

As children of God, we all have access to God, through Jesus Christ who willingly, obediently gave his life for us to redeem us from our sins. When we confess Jesus as our Savior and Lord, God sends his Holy Spirit to take up residence in our hearts. As believers, we all have the ability to hear the voice of God. (See John 10:2-4) It may not be an audible voice, but all of us have the promise of knowing and hearing his voice, at least in our thoughts. This fact alone does not make you or me crazy.

If you hear the voice of God, you already experience the joy of truly knowing the God of the universe who calls you his friend. If you are not currently hearing from God, it is not because he is unwilling to speak to you or because you are unable to hear him. God does not speak only to special clergy or prophets of old. God still speaks to his people today—all of his people—but not everyone takes the time to listen. Before you can hear God's voice, you must **believe** that you can hear it and **desire** to hear him speak.

One reason you may not hear God's voice could be that a sin stands in the way of your communication with God. An unrepentant heart can keep us from hearing the voice of God. Another reason that you may not hear God's voice could be that you have not quieted yourself enough to hear him speak. Sometimes, hearing God's voice takes practice. To hear God's voice, you must really listen. You must "*be still and know*" that he is God. (See Psalm 46:10) I encourage you to make a regular practice of sitting still in a quiet place, shutting out the world's noise, and listening attentively to the voice of God. Write down what you hear from God. Be careful to filter out your own thoughts and the voice of the enemy. Confirm, with God, the whispers you hear from him. The whispers of God will not encourage us to do things that are not wise. God's voice will align with his Word in Scripture every time. God does not contradict himself. Make sure that what you hear is in line with the character of God and God's Word from the Bible.

This book was written in the voice of God. You will hear the voice of God, Jesus, and the Holy Spirit speaking to you on these pages. My hope is that this book will ignite the passion in you for listening to God, and hearing his voice on a daily basis. I hope you, yourself, will take time to talk to God after reading each devotional. Use the devotional as a springboard into a personal "quiet time" with the Lord. Listen to what God has to say to you, personally, about each topic. Journal his whispers in a notebook and refer to them again, as needed. Confess any sin that God reveals in your life. Allow God to heal any brokenness that you may feel. Ask God to replace Satan's lies with the truth. Be inspired by God's love, encouragement, and instruction. Give God the praise and reverence he deserves. Thank him for his abundant blessings and faithfulness. Pray for God's presence, protection, wisdom, and direction in your life.

I have been a Christ-follower for many, many years; but the first time I actually listened for God's voice, and heard God speak to me, was a day that changed my life forever. My Christianity was no longer based on a religion, but a new-found "relationship" with the God I had been worshiping for years. It wasn't about a practice; it was about a person—Jesus Christ. About ten years ago, as I navigated my way through a period of depression, I needed to be reassured that there was more to life than what I had known and lived. I needed a reason to go on. I needed to know that I was a priority to someone and loved by someone. A friend of mine, who had been hearing God speak, encouraged me to listen for God's voice. My friend told me to talk to

God, as I would talk to a friend—have a two-way conversation with God—ask him questions and wait for his reply. My friend believed that God names each one of his children with his own unique name, especially for that person. I was encouraged to ask God, "What is your name for me?" and then listen for his reply.

First, I had to **believe that God would speak to me**. My friend assured me he would. Next, I desperately **wanted to hear God speak to me**. I wanted to know who I was to God and that he had a plan for my life. So one evening, I **escaped the noise** of my family, and retired to my bedroom where it was **quiet**. I began to **journal my thoughts to God** in a notebook. I asked God, "Do you have a name for me?" I listened intently, but heard nothing. I kept asking, but did not know what to expect, or how the answer would come to me. Would I hear an audible voice? Again I inquired of God, "What do you think of me? Who am I to you? What is your name for me?"

In my thoughts I heard, "DAUGHTER OF ZION." I wrote it down, but I quickly dismissed this name, not being able to relate to it at all. I asked God again, "What is your name for me?" Again, I paid attention to the voice in my head that replied, "DAUGHTER OF ZION." Once more, I thought it was a mistake. I couldn't identify with it. I did not understand the meaning of this name. I expected to hear something like, "my beloved one." A third time, I requested that God call me by the name he had for me. Yet again, God confirmed it—"DAUGHTER OF ZION." I heard it in my thoughts, and this time, the words took center stage in my head, displayed in all capital letters. Three times a charm—I decided to own the name I had heard three times inside my head. I knew it must be the name God had given me—but still, I did not understand it.

One way to confirm and comprehend what God says to us is to go to his Word. Using the concordance in my Bible, I began a two-hour search looking up all the verses and meanings I could find about the words "Daughter of Zion" and "Zion." I was very surprised to find more than 25 verses which contained the word "Zion." As I read each verse, a feeling of peace and joy came over me. I was overwhelmed with emotion. When I discovered the meaning of God's name for me, it made perfect sense. This name would, most likely, not mean the same thing to any other person; but it was everything I longed to be to God, and everything I desired to hear from God at that moment. Here are some examples of the identity I gleaned from the "Zion" verses: God is the King; I am his daughter (a princess). My Savior comes for me. My God, my King is with me. He has chosen me. He will save me. He, himself, will comfort me. He is delighted in me. He rejoices over me. I am sought after by God. I am no longer deserted and desolate. The Most High himself establishes me. I should rejoice and be glad. I am redeemed by the Lord. His dwelling place is in me. Everlasting joy will crown my head; sorrow and sadness will flee. The Lord will rebuild me. His name will be declared in me. He will turn back my enemies. God will show his favor to me.

That evening, God met me at the bottom of the pit I was in. He showered me with his loving kindness. He washed off the mud and lifted me up out of the pit. I connected with God in a way I never had before. God wasn't only an authority figure who lives in heaven, and disciplines me when I need it. He wasn't just a figure-head for me to worship. I had a new understanding that **God is alive**. God is a loving Father who cares about me, and wants to have a relationship with me. I felt special, wanted, and loved by God. I felt important to God. I was a priority to him. When I discovered how God felt about me, nothing else mattered. When I felt loved and wanted by the God of the universe, I had a new reason to live, and I was excited about what the future would hold for me. Not only did the name give me my identity in God's family, but it was pregnant with explanation and meaning of who I am to God, and who he is to me. It was exactly what I needed to know. This moment—the first time I really listened for God's voice and heard God speak to me—initiated a lifetime of running after God, and pursuing a more intimate relationship with my Savior.

After I knew I had heard God speak to me once, I believed and desired that he would speak to me again. I eagerly launched a new discipline of getting up early every morning to spend time in conversation with God, hoping that I would hear him speak again. I didn't hear God's voice every day, but as I consistently made the effort to communicate with God, I consistently heard his voice. It took commitment and practice—meeting with God in a quiet place every day, and emptying my mind in order to clearly hear his thoughts, his voice in my head. I kept a Bible close by, and used the concordance to find verses that would clarify and confirm what I heard God say to me. I purposely did *not* use this time for completing a formal Bible study. This early morning "quiet time" ritual was utilized solely for the purpose of speaking to God, listening to God's voice, and building a relationship with the Father, Son and

Holy Spirit. My foundation in Christ was fortified by the discovery of who he really is and who I really am in Christ.

The first priority in listening to God is to begin with prayer. I ask God for the ability to hear him speak. I ask God to help me recognize his voice. I start my quiet time by telling God that I desire to hear him speak to me. I pray that I will be able to discern his voice and thoughts from my own. I pray that I will hear him clearly. I ask God to protect me from distractions and confusion that come from my enemy, Satan. I ask God to reveal any sins that may stand in the way of hearing his voice. I repent of my sins and ask God to forgive me. I praise God for the gift of his Holy Spirit who lives inside me. Then, I am ready to begin my two-way conversation with God.

God already knows my thoughts, but I usually execute my side of the conversation by writing my thoughts and questions to God on paper or typing them on the computer. Sometimes I voice my thoughts and questions out loud to God in a conversational manner, while I am journaling them. Then, I wait to hear God speak. While I am waiting to hear God's voice, I journal every thought that pops into my head, no matter how miniscule or unimportant it seems. Before I know it, my pen is recording words on paper that I know are not my own cognitive concoctions. Yes, many times God speaks words to me that I long to hear, and I wonder, *Is this just my own self-soothing gibberish, or is this really God speaking to me?* But every time I re-read what I think I heard him say, I feel the reassuring peace and confirmation of knowing I am enjoying sweet fellowship with my wonderful God and Savior.

God's words are usually very loving and gentle, while at the same time, they exude a strength and firmness. God's words are convicting, not condemning. They are words of endearment and encouragement. God's words produce immeasurable peace within me. God's words bring me comfort and emotional healing. His words are always true and align with his Word in the Bible and his character every time. Sometimes God's words motivate me and stir me into action to carry out his will. Whenever I have acted on the promptings of the Holy Spirit of God, I have experienced an immeasurable, lasting joy in my life.

Pausing to listen for God's voice is vital. How can I hear God speak, if I am not leaving room in the conversation for him? Do not feel the need to fill the air with your own voice and thoughts all the time. Learn to become comfortable with the silence. Listen with both ears and everything in between. Clear your mind of all the clutter and obstructions. If random thoughts keep popping into your head—like, your grocery shopping list or your "to do" list for the day—quickly jot down these items, so that you won't forget them later, and then return to your still, expectant state of waiting on God. Focus on the topic of your discussion. Reiterate your questions or your comments to God. Then, write down the very next thought that comes into your mind. Keep writing the thoughts that enter your mind—all of them, no matter how common or strange they may seem. Sometimes you will find abundant meaning in the simplest expressions. Sometimes the thoughts that feel like our own thoughts are really the teachings and promptings of the Holy Spirit.

Don't be afraid to ask God for more clarification on something you have heard. Ask him to confirm that what you just heard was indeed from him. He may say it to you again, and verify it for you. Or you may need to seek confirmation in the Bible or from a trusted friend. God may confirm his whispers through the words of a song on the radio or a book you are reading. But check it out further. As many times as you ask for more confirmation, our patient God will authenticate what he has spoken to you. If you do not receive confirmation, it may not have been God's voice you heard.

Journaling is a practice that has proven effective and successful for me over and over in hearing the voice of God. Journaling is especially helpful when I want to revisit my communication with God at another time. When I experience times of drought, or not hearing God's voice, I return to the journal pages where I wrote down the whispers of God. I read through the pages, and they bring me comfort, encouragement, and a positive direction again each time I read them. I am able to reconnect with God, and remember what it sounds like to hear from him.

I wonder how many years God had been speaking to me, before I knew I could hear his voice. Now that I do know and listen to his voice, I will never be the same again. I pray God's best blessings for you, as you listen to the voice of God in this book, and take time on your own to hear the voice of God, Jesus, and the Holy Spirit speaking to you. It will be time well spent!

In the love and service of Jesus Christ,

Sindy

P.S.   If you have not yet accepted Jesus Christ as your Savior, and wish to do so, please see the last page of this book, which outlines a prayer of salvation. Read this prayer out loud. Accept the free gift of God's grace, and claim your salvation in Christ. There is nothing you can do to achieve your own salvation. Your redemption was already purchased on the cross by the death of Jesus. You simply need to confess your sins, and accept the free gift of salvation and eternal life from God. Begin your relationship with God today, and embark on a significant, meaningful adventure for the rest of your life here on earth, and for all of eternity.

INTRODUCTION

This book was written in the voice of God, as given to the author by the Holy Spirit of God, who lives inside each believer. As the author quieted her mind, tuned into the voice of God in her thoughts, and read God's Holy Scripture, she was inspired by the truth she heard and read, to write the words on these pages. You will hear the voice of God: Father, Son, and Holy Spirit, speak to you as you read each devotional.

You decide on the topic of the day for your "alone time" with God. You may need to ask for God's help in dealing with a current struggle or challenge. You may seek an uplifting word of encouragement from your loving Father in heaven. You may have an emotional wound that needs tending to. You may be called to be a witness to the saving grace of Jesus. You may desire to praise God for his goodness. Whatever you need or desire, the Holy Spirit, who resides in your heart, is waiting to hear from you. Your Counselor, Comforter, and Guide will speak the words you need to hear, exactly when you need to hear them. All you need to do is **listen** to him. God's love, wisdom, encouragement, and instruction are yours to obtain whenever you need them.

To receive the most benefit from this book, it is recommended that, as you spend "quiet time" alone with God each day, you practice the following:

- Find a place of solitude; away from noise and responsibilities
- Prepare your heart and mind with prayer
- Confess any sin that separates you from God, and ask for his forgiveness
- Ask God to lead you to the perfect devotional page for each day

- Ask God to speak to you, personally, through these pages
- Meditate on the Scripture and inspirational words that you read
- Pray that God will show you how to apply it to your life
- In a journal, write your own thoughts and questions to God
- Listen to God's voice in your thoughts, as the Holy Spirit speaks to you
- Write down the words, responses, and promptings you hear God speak
- Read his Word, the Bible, to confirm and enhance what you hear from God
- Test what you hear against the character of God and the Scriptures
- Filter out your own thoughts, as well as, the lies or doubts that Satan may plant in your mind to deceive you and confuse you
- Praise God for his loving words of encouragement, wisdom, and instruction
- Ask God for anything you desire, according to his will, in Jesus' name
- Believe that you will receive whatever you ask for in Jesus' name
- Commit to meeting with the Lord every day to experience an intimate relationship with The *Living* God, and receive your **Manna for Today**

Chapter 1

COME TO ME

*God invites us to draw near to him,
and he will draw near to us.*

"I am the living bread that came down from heaven. If a man eats of this bread, he will live forever. This bread is my flesh, which I will give for the life of the world." (John 6:51)

Bread from Heaven

You eat the food that spoils, and you are never satisfied, but God gives you the true bread from heaven that gives life to the world. Eat of the bread of life, and you will never hunger again. I am the bread of life. God has sent me to give you life. Feast on me and my words, and you will be satisfied. Believe in me, and you shall inherit everlasting life.

Your heart may feel empty and void. Your life may seem meaningless. Your hope may be diminished to a speck. Your flame of passion may have burned down to a glowing ember. Your zest for life may have evolved to apathy. Your spirit inside you may be slowly dying.

Come to me, my love. Run into my open arms. Believe in me, and I will satisfy all your needs. Let my Spirit fill your emptiness. Let me breathe the breath of life into your lungs. Let me fill your heart with a new passion for living. Believe in me, and find your reason to live. I am alive, and my Spirit lives in you. Do not be in despair—but find hope everlasting in my blood. I have died, so that you might live, and live abundantly. When you believe in me, you have the hope of eternal life. I will raise you up on the last day, and you will reign in heaven with me forever.

You no longer need to feed yourself with the food of mortals, but feast on the food of immortality when you choose the bread of life. I am the one my Father sent to save the world. I am the living bread that came down from heaven. I will give life to the world, and not just life, but life eternal. My Spirit gives you life anew. My Spirit is my gift to you when you repent of your sin, and believe in me.

Are you hungry? Eat and be satisfied. Are you thirsty? Drink and never thirst again. I have come to give you life. I live because of the Father who sent me. Feed on me and live. Feed on the bread of life, and live forever.

Then Jesus told them this parable: "Suppose one of you has a hundred sheep and loses one of them. Does he not leave the ninety-nine in the open country and go after the lost sheep until he finds it? And when he finds it, he joyfully puts it on his shoulders and goes home. Then he calls his friends and neighbors together and says, 'Rejoice with me; I have found my lost sheep.' I tell you that in the same way there is more rejoicing in heaven over one sinner who repents than over ninety-nine righteous persons who do not need to repent." (Luke 15:3-7)

Rejoicing in Heaven

My beloved one, you were lost. You wandered off on your own. You sought a different path than the one we were on. Your curiosity led you astray. Were you looking for thrills and adventure? Did you think there was a better life apart from me? Where were you going? Did danger entice you? Did you find what you were looking for? Was your life better apart from the one who created you, loves you, and calls you by name?

My child, you wandered away from the fold, so I eagerly left my throne to retrieve you. I left the others behind, and came after you. You are as valuable to me as all the other sheep in the flock. You were never out of my sight. I was always right there with you. My protection was your covering. You were lost, but now you are found. You were blind, but now you see. Your deaf ears have been opened. Your heart is soft and pliable. Let me mold you and make you after my will. Come home, my child. Return to me.

When you return to me, I place you on my shoulders joyfully, and carry you home. This calls for a celebration. The lost has been found. Come, friends and family. Rejoice with me. I have found my lost sheep. Let us sing. Let us dance. A feast has been prepared in your name. The angels cheer with me. There is rejoicing in heaven today. The lost has been found.

This is the assurance we have in approaching God: that if we ask anything according to his will, he hears us. And if we know that he hears us—whatever we ask—we know that we have what we asked of him. (1 John 5:14-15)

Approaching God's Throne

My child, come unto me. Approach me with the confidence of knowing that I hear what you ask me according to my will. If I hear you ask it, it will be done. There is nothing too big to ask of me; there is nothing too small to ask of me. Ask me for anything in my name, and I will do it. So many times, you do not ask. I stand waiting to hear from you, and you do not come to me.

I am ready to bless you with abundance, but you do not ask. There is forgiveness, healing, and redemption available, but you do not ask. I am capable of accomplishing the impossible, but you do not ask. Say to me, move that mountain, and it will be done. Part of your answer is in the asking. Being able to voice your dependence on me will grow our relationship by leaps and bounds. Understanding your role in our partnership is more than half the battle.

Too easily, you get swallowed up in life, and just simply forget I am here. Remember me each day. Think of me when your eyes open in the morning, before they close again at night, and all the time in between. You are never out of my thoughts. You are at the forefront of my mind. I begin my day with you, and end it just the same. I am with you always. Ask me for anything, my child. I will hear you, and answer you, according to my perfect will.

Approach my throne with confidence. You are the child of the King. There is no harm in asking. Do not be afraid to approach me about anything. You are dearly loved by me. I love the sound of your voice. I love to spend time with you. I created you to love you. Come to me today, my love. Ask me for whatever you desire. It is yours.

"Ask and it will be given to you; seek and you will find; knock and the door will be opened to you. For everyone who asks receives; he who seeks finds; and to him who knocks, the door will be opened." (Matthew 7:7-8)

Seek and Find

When you seek me, you will find me. My child, I am waiting for you to seek me. Seek me with your whole heart, and I will make myself known to you. Spend time with me away from the noise and distraction. In the quietness, I will reveal myself to you. In the still of the hour, you will hear my voice. I will give you the desires of your heart. Seek me earnestly to know me more deeply. I delight in you. I am eager to spend quality time with you.

Knock, and I will open up the floodgates of blessing for you. My door will never be closed to you. You are always welcome in my presence. My door is forever open to you; would you open the door of your heart to me? I stand at your door and knock. When you open your door, I will come into your heart and be your God. Let us enjoy sweet fellowship together.

Ask me for anything in my name, and I will give it to you. You have not, because you ask not. I have so much blessing to send your way, but you have not asked for it. There is healing available to you, but you have not requested it. My protection is accessible, but you do not expect it. My counsel is free, but you do not have time for me. Ask me, and it will be yours.

Behold, I stand at your door and knock. Would you invite me in? I want to embellish you with my love. I will cover you with mercy, and give you my peace. My forgiveness is yours to receive. You captivate me with your beauty, my love. My heart is open to you. My love for you is unconquerable. When you seek me, you will find me. I am right here. I have been here all the time. I am not going anywhere. Will you spend time with me?

"Enter through the narrow gate. For wide is the gate and broad is the road that leads to destruction, and many enter through it. But small is the gate and narrow the road that leads to life, and only a few find it." (Matthew 7:13-14)

The Narrow Gate

I am the narrow gate. I am the only way to the Father. Choose the narrow road that leads to life. When you lose your life for my sake, you will find it. Only a few are willing to walk the narrow road that leads to eternal life. Many choose the road that is broad. In the end, it leads to their destruction. Wide is that gate, because many will enter through it. Follow me, not the world. I will lead you to a life of abundance; a life in eternity with me.

The narrow road is the way the Father designed for you to be reconciled to him. This way has been prepared for you. My death on the cross has paved your way to the Father. I am the gate you will walk through to find your way back to the Father. Confess me as your Lord and Savior, believe God raised me from the dead, and you will be saved. The Holy Spirit, given to you by the Father in my name, seals your redemption. Not all will enter the gates of heaven, but only those who believe in me, and find their way to the Father through me.

I have marked out the way for you. Keep your focus on me. Many will come in my name and sound authentic; but I tell you, be forewarned, not all who call me Lord have come to speak the truth. Do not be misled by false teachers—ones who profess me as Lord, and yet, they contradict my Word. Be wise in discerning what you hear. Test everything against the Scripture. Be watchful for inconsistencies between what they say and what I have said. Tune into the Holy Spirit living inside you. He will direct you to all truth. He will remind you what I have said. I am the way, the truth, and the life. No one comes to the Father, but through me. Follow me, and find your life in me. Be reconciled to God the Father who knew you and loved you before he created the world. Spend eternity with us, and enjoy your inheritance.

He tends his flock like a shepherd: He gathers the lambs in his arms and carries them close to his heart; he gently leads those that have young. (Isaiah 40:11)

A Lamb in His Arms

My beloved child, I care for you as a shepherd cares for his flock. You are my precious lamb. I will gather you up in my arms, and carry you close to my heart. I love you so much that I will carry you around all day if you want me to. I have many sheep to tend to, but you are my prized possession. I will not let you wander away from the fold. I will gently lead you back to safety. The wolves will not have access to you because I hem you in. I protect you from your enemy.

Come to me, my lamb. I cherish the time we spend together. Let me overwhelm you with my love. Let me rejoice over you with singing. Let me teach you my ways. I will feed you in pastures of green. I will lead you to cool, quiet waters to drink. You will want for nothing. I take care of all your needs. You will never again go hungry or thirsty.

When you are tired from your journey, you may rest in my arms. In the shade of the trees, I will comfort you and ease your cares. Do not be anxious about anything. I am in control. Put your trust in me. I will carry your load, and lead you to the place I have prepared for you. Do not run ahead of me. You do not know the way. Follow me. I have cleared the road we will travel on. No traps will ensnare you; no barriers will divert you.

You are my child. I care for you deeply, and want to lead you in the way everlasting. Come to me, and find the abundant life you have been seeking. Believe in me, and you will spend eternity with me. Turn your eyes upon me, and do not look back. I will guide you in the way of wisdom. I will direct you into all truth. I am your good shepherd, and you are my precious lamb.

Therefore, brothers, since we have confidence to enter the Most Holy Place by the blood of Jesus, by a new and living way opened for us through the curtain, that is, his body, and since we have a great priest over the house of God, let us draw near to God with a sincere heart in full assurance of faith having our hearts sprinkled to cleanse us from a guilty conscience and having our bodies washed with pure water. (Hebrews 10:19-22)

Draw Near to God

I am your great high priest. I have opened a new way for you to enter the Most Holy Place, and approach the throne of God. My blood was shed as atonement for your sins. I am the sacrificial Lamb that was offered to God on your behalf, and I have cleansed you from all unrighteousness.

I have provided the way for you to be close to God. Your sins are forgiven. Your guilty conscience has been cleansed. Your body has been washed with pure water. You wear a new robe of righteousness. You have received the spirit of sonship; you have been adopted by God the Father as his own child.

Draw near to God with a sincere heart. Draw near to God, and he will draw near to you. Spend time in the presence of God. Offer up your praises to his holy name. Send up prayers of promise in my name. Live and walk by the Spirit of God that dwells within you. The Spirit will guide you into all truth. The Spirit will take from me what is mine, and make it known to you. Listen to the voice of the Spirit; it is the voice of your God. Listen and obey.

Draw close to God every day. By faith in me, you may approach God with freedom and confidence. You are God's child. He loves you more than you will ever understand. He loves you so much, he sent his own Son to pay the penalty for your sins. Your Father in heaven wants to be close to you. He looks forward to spending time with you. He has chosen you as his child because he loves you dearly. It is his pleasure and will that you have been saved by me. You are a child of the King. You may enjoy all the riches of his kingdom.

"For the Son of Man came to seek and to save what was lost." (Luke 19:10)

Seek and Save the Lost

Do you know where you are going? Have you lost your way? I came to find those who are lost and save them. Let me place you back on the right path, the path that leads to eternal life. I came to set the captives free, and restore the sight for the blind. What holds you captive today? Is it bondage to a repetitive sin? Does the enemy keep you repressed by his lies? Are you constrained by chains of bitterness and anger? Let me restore your vision.

There is no condemnation when you belong to me. I have paid the price for your freedom. You have been set free from your shackles. It is up to you to claim that freedom, and live a life of liberty. You do not need to be stuck in your sin. I provide the way out. You do not need to buy into the deception of the enemy. I have exposed his dishonest ways. Let go of the bitterness you once held on to. You are no longer blind to the ways of the evil one. The darkness gives way to the light. I am the light of the world.

I have sought you and found you. I have offered you the way to life. Will you follow me? Will you leave everything behind, pick up your cross, and follow me? I am the way to life everlasting. I am the way back home to the Father. I am the way to forgiveness. I am the way to freedom. I am the way to righteousness. I am the only way. Will you walk in it?

When you stumble and fall, I am here to pick you up, and set your feet on solid ground. The road is not always smooth, but I will walk by your side, and point out the obstacles in your way. When you follow where I lead you, I go first and prepare the way for you. You do not go alone. I am always with you. You once were lost, but now you are found. You were blind, but now you see clearly. When you lose your life, you will find it in me. Welcome home, my child. I never lost sight of you. You are always on my mind. You are my beloved child.

"For God so loved the world that he gave his one and only Son, that whoever believes in him shall not perish but have eternal life. For God did not send his Son into the world to condemn the world, but to save the world through him." *(John 3:16-17)*

Confirm Your Destiny

Sweetheart, I love you. I love you so much that I gave my Son, my only Son, for you. I did not send him to condemn the world, but to save the world. You are in the world. I sent my Son to save you. He traded his life for yours. Believe in my Son, and you will not perish in the pit of fire. Confirm your eternal destiny by confessing Jesus as your Lord. Believe in my Son. He gave his life for you. He died for your sins. He is the first born from the dead. He has been resurrected, and this guarantees your resurrection when you put your faith in Jesus Christ.

Does something stand in the way of your decision to finalize your future? Is it pride? Is it ignorance? Is it self-righteousness? Is it disbelief or doubt? There is no room for any of this foolishness in my kingdom. It is very simple. Believe that Jesus died for your sins, and that I resurrected him into heaven to sit at my right hand. He rules with me in heaven, and he pleads for your life.

Come to me, my child. I am your Father. I want to spend forever with you. Not a day goes by that I am not with you here on earth, but I want your eternal fate sealed. Every day is a blessing from me. Live each day as though it were your last. You do not know when the Son of Man will return. Will you be ready? Will you have made your decision for Christ when he returns? Do not take for granted each second you are alive. At any hour, your time may be up. Do you want to know for certain that you will go to heaven? Believe in the Lord Jesus Christ. Believe in me. Believe that I send my Holy Spirit to live in you when you commit yourself to me. Believe, and receive the free gift of eternal life with me. Believe in me, and experience the abundant life here on earth.

But God demonstrates his own love for us in this: While we were still sinners, Christ died for us. (Romans 5:8)

Christ Died for You

I love you, my child. I demonstrated my love for you by sending my Son to die for you—not just death, but death on a cross. Jesus Christ paid the ultimate price for your sin. While you were still powerless, he sacrificed himself for you. He gave his life in exchange for yours. As a result of his death, you have received reconciliation with me. Will you come to me?

You were born into the sin of Adam, but you have been made righteous through the obedience of Christ. Do not go on sinning then, when you have been baptized into Christ. You must die to your sin, as you have died and been buried with Christ. If you have died with Christ, you will also live again with him. No longer are you a slave to your sin. You have been freed from your sin through the death and resurrection of Jesus Christ. Count yourself, then, as dead to sin, but alive to God in Christ.

Do not be sold out to sin, but be sold out to life in me. There is a life to which you can obtain the freedom of righteousness. A life made free through the righteousness of Christ, is a life made free from sin and death. Live your life in obedience to me, just as Christ was obedient to me. Turn away from the life that calls you into unrighteousness. Stand up for what you believe in, and live a life of freedom.

I have loved you with a sacrificial love. I gave my Son's life for you. Will you now live for me? Live a life that is pleasing to me. Do not continue in self-indulgence, but indulge yourself in me. I am worthy of your time and energy. I will empower you to live into your freedom, the freedom that I give you. You are not bound by the chains of imprisonment. You have been set free. You are free to live your life accomplishing my work. I have created you to carry out my will. My plans are to prosper you. My plans are perfect. Live in the excellence of my will. I know what is best for you. My ways are higher than your ways. Your ways have not brought you the happiness that you seek. Abandon your ways. Live according to my will, and the joy of obedience will fill your heart. I love you, and I want the best for you. I am the best thing that will ever happen to you. Believe me.

For the wages of sin is death, but the gift of God is eternal life in Christ Jesus our Lord. (Romans 6:23)

My Gift to You

My beloved child, your sins have been forgiven. I accept your apology, and I pardon your iniquities. Now go and sin no more. You have been set free, so you are free indeed. You are no longer in bondage to sin. Do not give in to your sinful ways. You are being transformed daily into my likeness. I have overcome sin and death. I give you the power to overcome your temptations as well. I provide you a way out of the snares and traps you find yourself in.

Do not conform to this world, but be transformed by my Holy Spirit living within you. Listen to his voice. Heed his instructions. When you hear a "No," that means do not continue down the path you are on. Stop and listen. Listen and obey. Do not give in to your self-indulgent manner, but exercise restraint from within. This is a fruit of the Spirit I have given you. Taste the fruit of self-control. Taste and see that the Lord is good.

I was fully man when I walked the earth. It was only by the strength and power of the Holy Spirit of God that I remained without sin. You have that same Spirit living in you. Draw on the power of the Spirit within. Exercise strength of mind and strength of will. You know right from wrong. Always veer to the right. Do not allow the evil one to tempt you into doing wrong. You have access to the strength of God at all times, in all places, because it lies within you. Resist the devil, and he will flee from you. Stand firm, and do not give in. Walk upright in the Lord. Arm yourself with the sword of the Spirit, which is the Word of God. Fight the enemy with my Word. You are my great warrior. Receive the gift of my Spirit, and utilize the power from within. You will prevail. I have already won the war. There is nothing to fear. I have given you the gift of eternal life. Nothing can take that away from you. You are mine.

God, who has called you into fellowship with his Son Jesus Christ our Lord, is faithful. (1 Corinthians 1:9)

A Faithful Friend

My Father has called you into friendship with me. You are my friend if you do what I command. Everything I have learned from my Father, I make known to you. You know my plans, for I have called you my friend. In me, you have been enriched in every way. In your speaking and in your knowledge, you are an effective witness for me. Remain strong in the Lord as you eagerly await the second coming. God is faithful to renew your strength daily.

A friend loves at all times. A friend is faithful in all circumstances. There is a friend that sticks closer than a brother—I am that friend. I am dependable. I am devoted to you. I am trustworthy and loyal. I will not turn my face from you. When you walk through the fire, I go with you. Your hand in mine, I walk along side you through your struggles. I strengthen you and protect you from the evil one.

Come to me, my love. You are part of the family. Come to the table and dine with us. Let us break bread together and enjoy a common drink. I have broken my body for you. The one who feeds on me, the bread of life, will live because of me. My blood has been poured out for you. You will never thirst again. When you feast on my body, the bread, and my blood, the wine, you will be satisfied; and you will live forever with me. Remain in my love for all eternity.

Come to me, my darling. Let me embrace you with the love that you desire. Remain in my arms. I will delight in you. You will never be alone. I am always with you. I am a faithful friend. I will stay close to you. Whether you are asleep or awake, I am by your side. You are my precious one. It is for you that I gave myself as a living sacrifice. To you, I remain faithful to the end of the age. You are my living joy. I am your Savior and Lord.

But he who unites himself with the Lord is one with him in spirit . . . Do you not know that your body is a temple of the Holy Spirit, who is in you, whom you have received from God? You are not your own; you were bought at a price. Therefore honor God with your body. (1 Corinthians 6:17, 19-20)

One in Spirit

We are one in Spirit. You are united with me in the Spirit. Your body is my temple, my sanctuary. It is a refuge for my Spirit and yours. Honor me with your body. Do not defile it with too much food and too much drink. Do not unite yourself with another in sexual immorality. Do not put toxic substances into your body. Honor your body; it is a holy dwelling place for my Spirit.

My Spirit gives life. Be united with my Spirit, and live forever. Do not live according to the flesh, but according to the Spirit. Set your mind on the desires of the Spirit. Let your mind be controlled by the Spirit with life and peace. You are a daughter of God; therefore, you are led by the Spirit of God. Do not be led astray by your own fleshly desires, but delight yourself in the Lord, and he will give you the desires of your heart.

My Spirit helps you in your weakness. He intercedes for you in accordance with God's will when you do not know what to pray. When life has left you speechless and empty, my Spirit prays on your behalf as the mediator for your life. Do not grieve the Spirit. Do not hold onto anger and bitterness. Do not let unwholesome words proceed from your mouth. Instead, speak only what will build another up in Christ. Be kind and compassionate. Be ready to forgive in all circumstances. Live a life of love by the power of the Spirit within you. Be filled with the Spirit that God has given you. Be united with God through a life in Christ Jesus. Come to Jesus believing in the power of his name. It is for freedom that you have been set free. Be free to live life according to the Spirit that God has given you. You are one in the Spirit; you are one in the Lord. Your life is in the Spirit, where true life is found.

For I am convinced that neither death nor life, neither angels nor demons, neither the present nor the future, nor any powers, neither height nor depth, nor anything else in all creation, will be able to separate us from the love of God that is in Christ Jesus our Lord. (Romans 8:38-39)

Nothing Can Separate Us

My cherished daughter, nothing can separate you from my love. When you are in Christ Jesus, you are never far from me. My love for you will not be diminished by anything in all creation. No distance or span of time disconnects us. No power on the earth and no spirit of the air will overcome the love I have for you. Even death will not isolate you from me. Jesus has overcome death and the grave. Just as my Son joined me in heaven at my right hand, so you who believe in my Son will join me in heaven when you die.

You are my beloved child. I have adopted you as my own daughter. I have called you according to my purpose. I knew you before I created you. You have been conformed into the likeness of Christ. You are justified in his death. I have chosen you as my faithful one. You are under my protection. Nothing that comes up against you will triumph. Nothing and no one will stand in the way of my love for you.

My love for you is so enormous that I sent a member of my Holy Trinity to take up residence in you. Your body is the temple for my Holy Spirit. That is why I say that nothing can separate you from my love. I am with you at all times. I never leave you. I am available to you any time of the day or night. The depth of my love is revealed to you through the Spirit who lives inside you. Tap into my love by being in tune to my Spirit within you. Listen to my voice. The Spirit will teach you about Jesus. When you know Jesus, you know me as well. My Son died to bridge the expansion that existed between us when you lived in sin, but you have been reconciled to me, and nothing will break the bond that exists between us now. Nothing can separate us.

"When the Son of Man comes in his glory, and all the angels with him, he will sit on his throne in heavenly glory. All the nations will be gathered before him, and he will separate the people one from another as a shepherd separates the sheep from the goats. He will put the sheep on his right and the goats on his left. Then the King will say to those on his right, 'Come, you who are blessed by my Father; take your inheritance, the kingdom prepared for you since the creation of the world.'" (Matthew 25:31-34)

Are You a Sheep or a Goat?

Sheep go to my right, goats go to my left. Are you a sheep or a goat? Will you be on my right side or on my left? If you confess me as your Lord, and believe God raised me from the dead, you will be saved. You are my sheep. When Jesus comes again in his glory, you will be given your inheritance. You will take your place in heaven with me.

When you believe in me, you will aspire to be obedient like sheep. Delight yourself in me, and I will give you the desire to do good things. You will feed the hungry, give water to the thirsty, clothe the naked, care for the sick, provide shelter for the homeless, or visit those who sit in prison. When you do this for the least of these, you do it for me. As a believer, you are my sheep, and you will take your place on my right.

When you believe in me, you will live unselfishly—you will love unselfishly. If you have many things, and do not share them with the poor, you have no place with me. I have blessed you with much, yet you give only a little. To whom much is given, much will be required. Give with the measure that has been given to you. That includes love. I have given so much love to you, yet you give so little in return. Had I not given it to you first, you would have nothing to give; but since I have given you a great deal, you should be generous with what you have. Your gifts of love offered freely may make ready the way of salvation for the soul of another. You plant the seed. I will use your gifts and your love to draw another to me.

Imitate my love for you. Love generously. Love unconditionally. Love without expecting anything in return. Love one another as I have loved you.

*But Jesus immediately said to them: "Take courage! It is I. Don't be afraid."
"Lord, if it's you," Peter replied, "tell me to come to you on the water." "Come,"
he said. Then Peter got down out of the boat and walked on the water to Jesus.
(Matthew 14:27-29)*

Walk on Water

Do not be afraid. It is I. Come to me. Get out of the safety of your
boat and do the impossible. You can do all things through me. I will
give you strength. Nothing is impossible with me. You can walk on
water. You can heal the sick. You can restore sight to the blind. You can
make the lame walk, the deaf hear, the dumb talk. You will do even
greater things than these.

Do you have faith in me? Do you believe in me? Everything is
possible for him who believes. I will empower you and equip you to do
that which seems impossible. You can do anything you set your mind
to. Simply believe you can do it, and it will be done. If you have even
a speck of faith, you can move mountains.

Come to me, my child. Let me tell you who you are to me. You are
my precious one. You mean the world to me. I love you more than you
will ever understand. You are the child of the King. I am your strength
and your shield. I give you strength when you are weak. I protect you
in the battle. You will defeat the enemy when you are attacked. You
will slay the giant who stands in your way. I am your refuge and your
strength.

Have faith in me. I am the God of Abraham, Isaac, and Jacob. I
am the God of your forefathers, and I am your God too. I have blessed
you to be a blessing to the world. Come to me, and I will renew your
strength. I will prepare you to do what I ask of you. I will train you
in my ways, and send you out equipped for anything you may face. I
will supply you with your every need. Trust me. You are able to do
much more than you would ever imagine you could do, because my
power is at work within you. Walk to me on the water. It is only the
beginning.

"Come to me, all you who are weary and burdened, and I will give you rest. Take my yoke upon you and learn from me, for I am gentle and humble in heart, and you will find rest for your souls. For my yoke is easy and my burden is light." *(Matthew 11:28-30)*

Come to Me

Are you burdened by trouble or sorrow? Do you carry a load too heavy? Are you weary from your journey? Come to me. Rest in me. Let me lighten your load. Take my yoke upon you. Unite yourself with me. We will walk this journey together. I will bear the weight of your burdens. When you cannot continue, I will carry you. Give me all your worries and your concerns. I will take care of you. I do not grow tired or weary.

I will renew your strength. Put your hope and trust in me. I will get you through your trials. I will uphold you when you are too weak to stand. I will walk with you through the fire. You will not be burned. When you walk through the waters, they will not rush over you. Your trials are my trials. We will face them together. We will fight and win. We will remain strong together. I place my covering of protection on you. You are armed with my shield.

Though your journey seems long and tiring, I go with you. I am with you always. I am your light and your salvation. I will mark out the way for you. Do not wander away from the path I lead you on. Follow me, and I will not lead you astray. Stay close to me, and I will stay close to you. Listen to me. I have so much to teach you. Are you ready to hear me?

You know my voice. Listen to what I am telling you. I want to spend this time with you. I am devoted to you. I watch over you day and night. I know all things. My Spirit goes with you, and leads you into my light. Listen to my Spirit. I am the Counselor you need. Pour out your heart to me, and let me guide you down paths of righteousness for my name's sake. I will restore your soul. You need not carry your burdens alone. I am here. I will comfort you. Let go and let me.

But Jesus called the children to him and said, "Let the little children come to me, and do not hinder them, for the kingdom of God belongs to such as these. I tell you the truth, anyone who will not receive the kingdom of God like a little child will never enter it." (Luke 18:16-17)

Childlike Faith

Come to me, my child. My kingdom belongs to you. When you come to me as a child, I receive you with arms wide open. Your faith is new and fresh. It has not been altered and adulterated by the evil in this world. Your faith is pure and clean, not contaminated by lies and misconceptions. You look at me with childlike faith. You trust me completely with no questions asked. You submit yourself to my authority in blind obedience.

You do not know the future, nor do you need to. You know I will work all things together for your good because you love me. You live and walk by faith. You listen to me with attentive ears, eager to hear every word that flows from my mouth. My words are as sweet as honey to your soul. You hear my voice, because you are not distracted by the noise around you. You are focused on me alone.

You eagerly eat the food and drink I put before you, because you trust me. I lead you to pastures of green and fresh waters to sustain you. You run to me for safety, knowing that I will protect you. You climb into my arms when you need to feel my love. I do not need to chase you down to give you my affection. You enthusiastically soak up all the love I have to give you. When you are sad, you cry in my arms, and I comfort you with my love. I whisper in your ear, and everything is all right again.

You are my child, my precious child. Come to me any time. My kingdom belongs to you. I will receive you warmly. I am very fond of you. We will bask in the sunshine and play by still waters. I will tell you stories of great adventure. I will give you my love without limit. You are my treasure. You are priceless. Come to me, my child. I love you with all I have.

That if you confess with your mouth, "Jesus is Lord," and believe in your heart that God raised him from the dead, you will be saved. For it is with your heart that you believe and are justified, and it is with your mouth that you confess and are saved. (Romans 10:9-10)

Jesus is Lord

It is not enough that you call me Lord. You must also believe in me. Believe that God raised me from the dead. I am the one my Father sent to save the lost. Not only did I give my life on the cross for you, but my Father in heaven also raised me from the dead, so that the promise of eternal life would be fulfilled for all those who believe in me. When you confess me as Lord, and believe that God raised me from the dead, you will be saved. Everyone who calls on my name will be saved, and everyone who believes in me will be justified by faith.

Do you believe I am the Christ? I am the only way to salvation. The promise of eternal life has been fulfilled by my death and resurrection. It is not enough that I died in your place, but God has raised me from the dead, and seated me on the throne at his right hand. God placed all things under my feet, and made me Lord over everything. It is through your faith in me that you may approach God with freedom and confidence. I intercede for you as your great high priest.

God, who is rich in mercy, has made you alive in me. You are saved by the grace of God. Put your faith and trust in me. I live in your heart by the Spirit of God who lives within you. You have been sealed for redemption. I will strengthen you with power from on high. You have been crucified with me. You are dead to your sins and alive in my Spirit. Live your life as my victorious child. I have won the battle for your soul. You belong to me. You are God's workmanship, created to do good works. Live in the power of the Spirit of God. Tune in to the Spirit, and know me more intimately. I will reveal myself to you through the Spirit.

"Here I am! I stand at the door and knock. If anyone hears my voice and opens the door, I will come in and eat with him, and he with me." (Revelation 3:20)

Open the Door

I am here. I stand at the door of your heart and knock. Do you hear my voice? I am calling out to you. Will you let me in? Invite me in to your heart, and I will draw near to you. Be sincere and repent. Ask forgiveness for your sins and turn away from your corrupt behavior. Believe in me and sin no more.

When you invite me into your life, you will lose your life, but you must lose your present life before you will find new life in me. The old way of doing things did not get you your salvation. Your salvation comes from confessing your sins and believing in me. I am the only way to the Father. I am the way, the truth, and the life. You cannot find your way to the Father, except by me. Follow me, and I will lead you down the path of true life.

Open the door. Let us break bread together. I will dine with you and you with me. When you come to me, you will never hunger again. I am the bread of life. I am all the nourishment you need for your soul. Believe in me, and you will never be thirsty. I give you the living water, a water which will become in you a spring of water welling up to eternal life.

Here I am. Do you hear my voice? I am knocking. Will you open the door? You are my beloved child. I will prepare a feast for you in my name. Spend time with me. I want to hear what you have to say. Listen to me and learn. I have great plans for your life. I need your help in my kingdom. I will prepare the way for you. I will equip you for the work I have laid out for you to do. You will accomplish all the things I ask of you, because you put your trust in me. I will give you strength and power when you put your hope in me. You will soar on wings like eagles. I am your helper. I am yours, and you are mine. We'll work together.

The Word became flesh and lived for a while among us. We have seen his glory, the glory of the one and only Son, who came from the Father, full of grace and truth. (John 1:14)

Full of Truth

When I walked among you as a man, you did not know me. I did not receive a warm welcome in my hometown; but I tell you the truth, you have seen the glory of the Lord. I am my Father's Son. I came into this world to seek and save the lost. Those who do not recognize me will remain lost forever, but all who receive me and believe in my name have the right to become my Father's children, born of God.

Too many of you live in the darkness of a life without a Savior, but I have come to expose the darkness, and replace it with the light of my truth. The truth is, without me, you will perish. Without me, you will not live eternally. There is only one way to receive the gift of everlasting life—believe in me. I do not condemn you, but offer you life. Come, my child. Step into the light. Let it be seen plainly that you belong to me. My glory will shine in you.

Today I extend the favor of my grace to you. Seek me, and you will find me, when you seek me with all of your heart. My blessing is in your hands. Know me, and you will know my Father also, for we are one. Walk with me; I will illuminate your way. Listen to me, and carry my wisdom with you wherever you go. I lead you down the path of light. In me there is no darkness. The light of my truth will testify to those who remain in the shadows. I am the one and only Son of God. I am the only way to the Father. When you have seen me, you have seen my Father. I will make him known to you.

Leave the darkness behind you, and move into the light of an abundant life in me. Call on my name, and I will be your Savior. Believe in me, and you will become a child of the King. Draw near to me, and I will draw near to you. The way is narrow; now walk in it. I am by your side. I will never leave you.

Chapter 2

FOLLOW ME

The way is narrow that leads to the path of life.
His words are a lamp for our feet.

"Whoever serves me must follow me; and where I am, my servant also will be. My Father will honor the one who serves me." (John 12:26)

Serve Me

In order to serve me, you must spend your days walking with me. Follow me so closely that you actually walk in the dust my feet stir up. Stay close to me, and do as I do. Learn from me; there is much for me to teach you. Pay attention to my stories; the greatest lessons to be learned dwell within these sayings. I am my Father's Son. I will do the will of my Father in heaven. Follow me closely, and discern the will of my Father for you. I will make it known to you through the Holy Spirit God has given you in my name.

Serve me wholeheartedly. My Father will reward you for serving me. Serve with the strength God provides, for it is God who works in you. Serve with humility. Serve others with my love. Consider others better than yourself. Look to the interest of others before you look to your own interests. Humble yourself before the Lord, and serve him with gladness. Your obedience to the will of God is critical. When you are called, obey. Serve without grumbling, but be joyful in your service to the Lord.

Be watchful and dressed for service. When I call on you, you should be ready. Do not let me find you asleep, when I have called you to assist me. You have been given much, and much will be required of you. Whatever I have called you to do, work at it with all your heart. You are working for me. Your reward is your inheritance. Follow my lead, work diligently, and receive your reward. It is by knowing me and believing in me that you have this opportunity to serve me. Be mindful of what you do, and do it by the grace of God whose Spirit lives in you. Serve me and follow me. Follow me and serve me.

"The watchman opens the gate for him, and the sheep listen to his voice. He calls his own sheep by name and leads them out. When he has brought out all his own, he goes on ahead of them, and his sheep follow him because they know his voice." (John 10:3-4)

Listen and Follow

I have opened the gate for you. I am calling you home. Do you hear my voice? I have called out your name. Listen and follow. I have prepared a way for you. I will go on ahead of you. It's your job to follow. Listen to my voice and follow me. My voice is tranquil. My voice is confident. It exudes peace. You know my voice. Can you hear me now? You must be still. My voice is not loud. It may not be audible for you. You may hear me only in your thoughts. You will have to find a quiet place in order to hear my voice. You will have to be still and know that I am God. Find a place where you can filter out the noise and distraction. Even the static of your own thoughts must be dispelled.

Allow me to speak. Do not feel you need to fill the air with your own voice every time we meet. Be still and listen to mine. It is important for you to record what you hear. Write down my words to you. You will need to refer to them when you lose your way, just as you have my words in the Bible. When I speak to you, instruction will be on my lips. A kind word, a necessary truth, a look into my character—these are the types of things you will hear from me. I will speak the truth in love, and you must listen.

I will not condemn you or shame you. I will not accuse you. Those thoughts are of my enemy. Quickly discard those thoughts. The voice of my Holy Spirit may convict you at times. Do you see how that is different from condemnation? There is now no condemnation for those who are in Christ Jesus. You know my voice. I love to hear yours, too. I hear everything you have to say to me. I know your thoughts before you communicate them, but it is important for you to speak them to me. It is in this two-way communication that our relationship is developed and maintained.

There is a time to speak and a time to listen. Be conscious of this and practice it. We must be intentional about our time together. We must make it a priority in our day. Talk to me any time you like. I am always with you and always ready to listen. The length of time we spend talking to each other is not as important as the effort that is made to achieve this on a daily basis. We can speak to each other all day long, but there are times when we need to meet away from the noise. Be vigilant about meeting with me. Listen and follow.

A good name is more desirable than great riches; to be esteemed is better than silver or gold. (Proverbs 22:1)

Your Name

My child, your parents named you when you were born, but I have given you my name for you as well. You are the child I delight in. I have a different name for each of my children. Each one should seek me for the name I have declared for him or her. The name I assign each of you is as unique as the person who wears it. Your name was engraved on my palms before you were conceived in your mother's womb.

You are my child, my heir. You belong to me. I wanted you, so I created you. You were no accident. Your name defines you. You are much like my Son, Jesus. You are strong, yet tender. You are more precious than rubies, more valuable than silver or gold. You are royalty. Your name is better than fine perfume and more desirable than great riches. I have called you by name. You are mine.

When I call your name, listen to my voice, and follow me. You know the sound of my voice. I speak to you in your thoughts. I speak to you softly and gently, as if in a whisper. You must quiet yourself and your mind in order to hear me speak. When you hear my voice, I ask you to follow me. Obey my voice and my commands. I will lead you; I go ahead of you. Follow me. Follow the sound of my voice. I will not lead you astray. I will lead you to the Father. He knows your name. You are his child.

Where I lead you, you must follow. I have your best in mind as I lead you. I see and know everything—much more than you will ever see and know. I know the best way for you. Walk in the way I guide you. Do not stray from the path I place you on. I came to give you a full life. Live your life for me. Find the fulfillment of my promises when you follow me.

Do you not know that in a race all the runners run, but only one gets the prize? Run in such a way as to get the prize. (1 Corinthians 9:24)

Run for the Prize

My blessed one, do not run ahead on your own. Your efforts are futile without me. When you follow your own plan, your efforts are in vain. The unsuccessful results will eventually lead to your disqualification in the race. Seek me first, and you will do even greater things than I did on this earth. I have a plan. You know my plan is for your good.

You do not see the grand picture as I do. You will know my plan in due time. I will let you in on exactly what you need to know for the mile marker you are at. For now, put one foot in front of the other, taking my hand as I lead you. The hare that raced ahead found he became weary, needing rest, and wound up losing the race. The tortoise, which pressed forward at a steady pace, crossed the finish line first, and found his success. Do not race ahead of me, but press on consistently with your focus on me.

Run with perseverance. Run with determination and resolve. Do not run aimlessly. Focus on the prize ahead of you—eternal life with me. Do not look to the left or to the right at those running alongside you. Do not compare yourself to anyone else. Your race has been marked out by me. Keep your focus on me. Run for the prize—me! Live with purpose. Live with intentionality. Live victoriously. Keep running.

"You will seek me and find me when you seek me with all your heart. I will be found by you," declares the Lord, "and will bring you back from captivity." (Jeremiah 29:13-14a)

Find Me, Find Freedom

I do not hide myself from you. You simply need to look for me, and you will see me. Look to the skies and find me in the sunset. Look to the mountains and find me in the majestic peaks. Look to the seas and find me in the surge of the tide. Look to the trees and find me in the autumn leaves. Anywhere you look, I will be found by you. I dwell not only in the beauty of my creation, but I have made my home in you. You need to look no further than your own heart to find me. Seek me. Find me. I will set you free from the ties that bind you.

Although you make yourself scarce to me at times, I am always with you. Whether you see me or not, I am there. Recall any memory you desire, and if you really search for me, you will find me in it. Believe my words, and they will be accomplished. Put your hope and trust in me; I will not disappoint you. Call on me and pray to me, and I will listen to you.

You have been held captive by my enemy. Seek me, and I will set you free. No longer will you be bound by the chains around your neck. I hold the key to your release and happiness. You have been imprisoned so long, you do not remember the feeling of liberty. Pursue me, and you will find me. You do not have to go far. I am here with you. Look into your heart, and see my fingerprints. I formed you; you are mine. Follow me, and I will set you free.

Come and sit with me for a while. I will listen to you, and fill you with my love for you. The void you have felt in your heart will disappear. Your emptiness will be filled with all of me. When you know me, you will believe me. Ask me, and I will answer you. You know my voice. Listen to my voice, and discover who I am. Know me and understand me better. Listen to me and hear the truth. The truth will set you free.

Now devote your heart and soul to seeking the Lord your God. (1 Chronicles 22:19a)

Seek Me with All Your Heart

When you seek me with all your heart, you will find me. Give your heart and soul over to the mission of searching for me. You need not travel far, for I am with you. Simply look into your own heart and you will find me. I am there. I live in you. You can find me anytime you look. I hear every word you say; I see everything you do. I listen when you speak to me. I am right there beside you. I stick closer to you than a friend.

Seek me, and you will lack nothing. I hear your cries. I will deliver you from your troubles. I will protect you and provide for you. You will find your refuge in me. I will save you when your spirit has been crushed. I will deliver you from the grip of the enemy. When your soul is in despair, I am there to lift you up, and wipe away all your tears. My compassions do not fail. I understand your pain. I know your grief. I have experienced the same rejection. I have endured the scorn and suffered the shame.

However, the day is coming when every knee will bow to the one who is seated on the throne. My Son, the Lamb of God, purchased your salvation with his blood, and conquered death. He is seated on my right hand. I have prepared a place for you in heaven also. You will spend eternity with me, and I will make everything new. I will be your God, and you will be my people.

When you seek me with all your heart and soul, I will be found by you. I am not a god who is a figure carved out of stone. I am the living God, and I live in you. You will find me when you search for me earnestly. I am like a hidden treasure in the depths of your soul. Get in touch with my Spirit, and you will know me also. Your life will be rich when you walk in the Spirit. The wealthy man has nothing on you. Money and fame do not buy happiness, but true joy awaits you when you sincerely pursue me. I will make myself known to you.

"Again, I tell you that if two of you on earth agree about anything you ask for, it will be done for you by my Father in heaven. For where two or three come together in my name, there am I with them." (Matthew 18:19-20)

I am with You

I love it when my children get together to pray. I am glorified in the presence of believers who are gathered in my name. When you join with another in prayer, two or three minds are united in me. Each of you has the power of effective prayer on your own, but when two or three of you pray in agreement, the power of your prayer increases one hundred times or more. I want you to know that I am with you when you gather to pray, and I will give you what you ask for.

I am delighted when two or three come together in my name for any reason. Whether it is worship, Bible study, mentoring, prayer, singing, or fellowship, I am there with you. It reminds me of the Trinity relationship. I have given you the glory that the Father gave me. I have prayed that all believers will be one, just as my Father and I are one. My Father is in me, and I am in you.

It is the greatest mystery for you to comprehend. Father, Son, and Holy Spirit—we are three distinct entities, and yet one God. Do not spend your time proving my ways. This mystery is not one that you will ever understand completely. My ways are higher than your ways, but as you seek to know each person of the Trinity better, your knowledge will increase, and understanding will be your blessing. You do not have to understand me fully to believe in me fully. This is where the faith and trust comes in. Just "know" that I am God. I am in control. I am trustworthy. I am with you. When you believe in me, you have the gift of the Holy Spirit living inside you. As you grasp this idea, you will better understand our relationship. I am in you, just as my Father is in me.

But you are a chosen people, a royal priesthood, a holy nation, a people belonging to God, that you may declare the praises of him who called you out of darkness into his wonderful light. (1 Peter 2:9)

Follow Me

My chosen one, you belong to me. I am the light of the world. Follow me, and you will never walk in darkness. Follow me, and you will have the light of life. Believe in me, and the light of my truth will be alive in you and guide you. I am the way, the truth, and the life. I am the way to the Father. I shine my light into the dark corners, and expose the truth. When you follow me and believe in my name, you will have the light of life. You will know the truth, and the truth will set you free from your captivity in this dark world.

When you have the light of the world, you have the light of life. I am the Son of God. I have sent my Spirit to guide you into all truth. When you walk in the light, you walk in the truth. The truth is that I am my Father's Son. I am the way my Father has provided for you to be reconciled to himself. I have laid down my life willingly and obediently for you. I gave my life in exchange for yours, so that you may have the light of life. If you have seen me, you have seen the light. If you know me, you know my Father as well.

I am the light of life. When you walk in me, there will be no darkness. For the darkness cannot co-exist with the light. The deceiver will not be found in my presence. The light repels the darkness. My light causes the blind to see. Your eyes have been opened because of the light. You know the truth. You see the ways of the evil one. You recognize his schemes. No longer will you sit in darkness. His prison will no longer contain you.

You have turned from the darkness and stepped into the light. When you believe in me, you have the light of life inside you. My Holy Spirit is your personal light. He will guide you into all truth. He will teach you my ways, and remind you what I have said in my Word. You need not wonder about anything in life. The Holy Spirit takes from me what is mine, and makes it known to you.

My truth lives in you. My Spirit is alive in you. When you walk in the Spirit, you are alive in the Spirit. Live by my Spirit, and you will have the light of life. Never again will you walk in darkness. How much more abundant is life, than life in the Spirit? You will never hunger and thirst again. You have all you need, because you have me. Follow me. I will light your way.

Then he said to them all: "If anyone would come after me, he must deny himself and take up his cross daily and follow me. For whoever wants to save his life will lose it, but whoever loses his life for me will save it." (Luke 9:23-24)

Deny Yourself

My dear one, you will be saved by my grace. When you give your life to me, you will be saved. Lose your life for my sake, and I will save it. This does not make sense to you, but it makes perfect sense to me. Just as I have laid down my life for you, I ask you to lay down your life for me. Leave the old life behind, and embrace the new life ahead. Leave your worldly comforts behind. Do not look back, but take up your cross daily, and follow me. When you submit yourself to me daily, you will have the life I intended for you.

It is a mystery that when you lose your life you will save it, but you were already lost when I found you. Follow me, and I will save you from eternal destruction. I am the only way to eternal life with the Father. In order to follow me, you must deny yourself. Renounce the life you once had, and surrender your life to me. When you give yourself fully to my calling, you will give up your former ways.

Follow my example. I willingly and obediently gave up my life to save yours. When I submitted myself to the will of God, I took up my cross, and died on the cross so that your life could be spared. We all have crosses to bear. Some are more difficult than others. Some crosses require complete sacrifice. Willingly take up your cross, and be obedient to your calling. I would not ask you to do something I have not done myself. When you take up your cross and follow me, you will be saved. Lose your life for my sake, and find your new life in me. You must deny yourself to follow me. Believe in me, follow me, and you will be saved.

Do not conform any longer to the pattern of this world, but be transformed by the renewing of your mind. Then you will be able to test and approve what God's will is—his good, pleasing and perfect will. (Romans 12:2)

Be Transformed

My beloved, you are in the world, but no longer of the world. You belong to me. You are a member of my kingdom now. When you gave your life to me, you signed up for a complete makeover. God sent you the Holy Spirit in my name. The Spirit of God takes up residency within you. He ignites a fire of passion in you for me and the work of my kingdom. In the process of living for me, and doing my work, you will be changed.

You are now one with the Spirit. You will be transformed by my Spirit; much like a caterpillar becomes a butterfly. Bit by bit, lesson by lesson, your life will be renovated. Be in tune with my Spirit, listen to my voice, remain in my Word, your mind will be renewed. You will see glimpses of my will for you. Examine my will. Test it against my Word. When you see that my will and my Word are in alignment, you will be eager to support my perfect plans. My plans are to prosper you, not to harm you.

With the knowledge and wisdom my Spirit gives you, your heart will sing a new tune. You will experience a lasting joy like no other. The joy comes from the assurance of a life with me. Not only an abundant life here on earth, but also a place in heaven with me for all eternity. You will experience the peace of knowing that I am in control. You do not need to worry about anything. I will take care of you.

There will be storms in this life, but I am with you in the storm. I stand up with you, and command the wind and the waves to cease. I bring peace to your days and confidence to your spirit, even in the midst of the tempest. I work all things together for your good. The storms are used in your transformation process. Head into the wind and be transformed.

Therefore, there is now no condemnation for those who are in Christ Jesus, because through Christ Jesus the law of the Spirit of life set me free from the law of sin and death. (Romans 8:1-2)

No Condemnation

You are free. Jesus Christ has set you free, so you are free indeed. You are free from condemnation. Your death sentence has been paid by my Son, the Savior of the world. The penalty for your sin is death. That debt has been paid on your behalf. No longer will you be sentenced to die for your transgressions. The Lamb of God has taken away the sins of the world. He died in your place, so that you might live.

Now live according to the Spirit, not according to the flesh. You are a new creature in Christ Jesus. Do not give in to your human desires, but set your mind on what the Spirit desires. You are one with the Spirit of God who lives inside you. Now live by the Spirit that has set you free. Be controlled by the Spirit. You are now dead to sin and alive because of his righteousness. The Spirit gives you life.

Turn away from your own wickedness, and carry out your days in uprightness. You have received the Spirit of adoption. You are my child. You have been set free. Now be conformed to the likeness of my Son, Jesus. Let the Spirit transform you in the process of your sanctification. Your life is dedicated to me. You will be a blessing in my kingdom. You are set apart for a higher calling in Christ Jesus. Live into that calling, and follow me in obedience. Put your trust in me, for I will lead you on paths of righteousness.

Leave behind the former life, and start fresh your new life in me. You have been washed by the blood of the Lamb. You are holy and blameless in my sight. Remain pure and true. Do not be deceived by the evil one. Do not believe the lies of the enemy. You are my child, and I love you. I have chosen you. I created you. I will love you to the end of your days on earth, and for all of eternity. I have a purpose for your life. I have an assignment for you in my kingdom. You are mine.

"So I say to you: Ask and it will be given to you; seek and you will find; knock and the door will be opened to you. For everyone who asks receives; he who seeks finds; and to him who knocks, the door will be opened." (Luke 11:9-10)

I am Here

Do not forsake the act of praying, even praying together. It is not an old-fashioned practice to be left to the clergy or church staff. You don't even need to pray inside the walls of the church building to be effective. Anytime two or more are gathered together in my name, anywhere, to pray, I am with them. When two of you agree about anything you ask me for, I will do it for you. This is one of the keys to effective prayer, pray with one another in the faith.

It is a privilege to pray for one another. Some countries of the world do not allow this practice in public. In those places, Christians literally have to go to their closets to send off prayers to me. Some would be sentenced to death for worshipping me in their corner of the earth, but if you live in a country that has established the freedom of religion, praying may be allowed in private or in public. You have the ability to practice your faith in your home and on the street corners if you wish. You may proclaim me from the mountaintops without being arrested.

Just as a husband and wife are joined together in marriage to be one flesh, so you are joined to me. You are my bride. You and I are one. I am with you always. I am here when you pray. I am pleased when you set aside time to pray to me. Let your requests be made known to me. No ask is too small. No ask is too big for me. I will deliver what you ask for when you pray in my name. Just ask for it, and it will be yours.

When you pray with another, put his or her interests ahead of your own. Become one in spirit and purpose. My joy is complete when you are like-minded in Jesus Christ. Imitate Christ by taking on the mind of a servant. Be obedient to the prompting of the Spirit. Yield yourself in submission to me. Join together in harmony as you pray in the Spirit. Come together, and devote yourselves to prayer. Just ask. I will open up the floodgates of heaven.

For, "Whoever would love life and see good days must keep his tongue from evil and his lips from deceitful speech. He must turn from evil and do good; he must seek peace and pursue it. For the eyes of the Lord are on the righteous and his ears are attentive to their prayer, but the face of the Lord is against those who do evil." (1 Peter 3:10-12)

Pursue My Peace

My dear believer, when you decide to follow me, you must turn from evil and do good all of your days. You must lay down your life, take up your cross, and follow me. Discard your former ways, and pursue my peace. Get rid of all lying and cheating. Do not deceive anyone with your words. Do not use foul language and malicious words. Do not be mean and spiteful. Abandon your sinful ways, and act in a respectable manner.

Pursue my peace in all you do and say. Do not pay back an evil thing that was done to you, but offer a blessing as your weapon of choice. In so doing, you will inherit a blessing. Do not offend those who have insulted you, but choose words that will build up your offender. Seek peace in the middle of strife. Pursue my peace. Chase after the truth with enthusiasm. I observe those whose walk is blameless. I listen to the prayers of the righteous.

Where evil is present, you will not find me. I turn my face from the wicked. I oppose the sinful nature, but those who seek my peace, will receive a blessing from me. Even if you must suffer for doing my good, choose the better way. Live in harmony with one another. Be loving and compassionate. Be sympathetic and humble. I resist arrogance, but give grace to the meek. You will be blessed with your inheritance.

Love your adversary, and pray for those who mistreat you. Bless the ones that irritate you, and benefit the ones that detest you. You will be called my sons and daughters, when you respond to the behavior of the world, with the ways of God. If you desire a good life and good days, you will pursue my peace. The peace I give you will exceed your expectations.

This is the message we have heard from him and declare to you: God is light; in him there is no darkness at all. If we claim to have fellowship with him yet walk in the darkness, we lie and do not live by the truth. But if we walk in the light, as he is in the light, we have fellowship with one another, and the blood of Jesus, his Son, purifies us from all sin. (1 John 1:5-7)

Walk in the Light

My blessed children, if you believe in me, you will walk in the light. I am the light of the world. Do not remain in obscurity when you have a good light to follow. If you claim that you are with me, yet you walk in the shadows, you deceive yourself and others. Do not acknowledge me as your Lord if you do not intend to follow where I lead you. Step out of the darkness and into the light. Walk by faith, not by sight. Live in the truth of the light.

God is light. When you walk in the light, you walk in God. How awesome is it that you may experience a close companionship with the King of the universe. I call you my friend. When you remain in me, I will remain in you. Obey my Word and my Father's love is perfected in you. Be true to yourself, and walk in the light, as I am in the light. Confess your sins, follow me, and I will cleanse you from all unrighteousness. When you follow me, my truth will be seen in you.

What a witness you will provide as you follow me into the light of God. Always be prepared to be a witness to my light. Be ready to share the reason for your hope. Be gentle and respectful as you claim your stake in me. You do not want to extinguish the glowing ember I have ignited in another. Your passion for me will increase a flame in someone else. Before you know it, another will be on fire for the Lord, and my light goes on and on. You will experience the fellowship of those who think like you when you surround yourself with my disciples. Where two or three come together, I am there. How sweet is the aroma of a brotherhood of believers?

"But be very careful to keep the commandment and the law that Moses the servant of the Lord gave you: to love the Lord your God, to walk in all his ways, to obey his commands, to hold fast to him and to serve him with all your heart and all your soul." (Joshua 22:5)

Hold Fast to Me

My darling one, I hang on to you. I am never far from you. You are always on my radar. I have my eyes on you. I hold you close to my heart. Will you hold fast to me? Cling to me when you are uncertain. Stick close to me when you are in trouble. Hang on to me when you are afraid. I will not let go of you. You are in the grip of my grace. Your life rests in my capable hands. Hold fast to me, in both good times and bad.

Serve me with gladness. Your heart and soul belong to me. Serve me in the fullness of all your heart. Wait on me. I am the anchor of hope for your soul. Give to me with the measure I have given to you. I have laid down my life for you. Will you lay down your life for me? Will you devote your whole heart to me? Keep my commandments. Love me with all of your heart, soul, mind, and strength. Love your neighbor as you, yourself, have been loved by me. Submit your heart to me and your soul to my Spirit. My Spirit lives in you.

Follow my example, and walk in my ways. You are in this world, but you are a stranger to it. When you devote yourself to me, you do not live as the world lives. Consider yourself an alien, unfamiliar in the land. Do not buckle under the pressure the world applies. I will protect you and equip you with my strength. Proudly wear the breastplate of righteousness I have given you, and shield your heart from the arrows of the enemy. Carry the sword of the Spirit in your right hand. Hide my Word in your heart, and draw it out when you need it. I go with you in the battle. I have prepared your feet with the gospel of peace. You will never walk alone. In every situation, hold fast to me, and I will hold fast to you.

As Jesus was walking beside the Sea of Galilee, he saw two brothers, Simon called Peter and his brother Andrew. They were casting a net into the lake, for they were fishermen. "Come, follow me," Jesus said, "and I will make you fishers of men." At once they left their nets and followed him. (Matthew 4:18-20)

Come, Follow Me

Do you hear me calling your name? Listen to the sound of my voice. I am calling you. "Come, follow me." I see that you are looking for direction, and I know the way. I am the way. Follow me, and you will be doing the will of my Father. He sent me to save you. My Father desires that all his children would return to him. I am the only way back home to the Father. I will go ahead of you and prepare the way. You come after me, and walk in the way I have made ready.

I see that you are busy working. You are accomplishing the tasks of the day. Come, follow me. I have laid out a new path for you. I have a place for you to work in my kingdom. There are many who have drifted off course. I will send you, just as my Father sent me, to seek and save the lost. You cast your nets into the sea but they come up empty. Follow me, and the work I give you will bring you much joy and fulfillment. Lives will be changed.

When I call you, do not tarry. Quickly act upon my instructions, as Peter and Andrew did, and we will lose no time. At the sound of my voice, these men dropped their nets at once and followed me. They didn't even know me. They left everything to chase after me. You know me, and yet, you are hesitant to follow where I lead. I will not steer you off course.

I call you because I love you. There is nothing more important than the work I have for you. Respond to the sound of my voice. You know who I am. My Father has given me charge over you. I will guide you on the path of righteousness for my name's sake. The path I call you to leads upward to my Father. Do not look the other way as if you do not hear me. I will not give up on you. I have called you and commissioned you to do my Father's work.

Not that I have already obtained all this, or have already been made perfect, but I press on to take hold of that for which Christ Jesus took hold of me. Brothers, I do not consider myself yet to have taken hold of it. But one thing I do: Forgetting what is behind and straining toward what is ahead, I press on toward the goal to win the prize for which God has called me heavenward in Christ Jesus. (Philippians 3:12-14)

Press On

My dear one, you are in an important race. Do not look back. Do not think about what is already behind you. Whatever you have lost is for your gain. When you gave up the life you knew, you gained a greater life in me. Take hold of that for which I have taken hold of you. Focus on what is ahead of you. Press on. Win the prize for which God has called you to. Make forward progress in your heavenward journey. God is calling you in his direction. Do not look back. Exert yourself on the upward path.

Do not let anyone interrupt you and keep you from following the truth. Confusion does not come from me. Be aware of the enemy's persuasion. He can distract you and disqualify you from finishing the good race you were running. Keep your focus on the prize. Your full attention is required. Do not be easily swayed by the onlookers who may mock you. They do not see or understand what they have been called to. They do not listen to my voice.

This is not a relay race, in the fact that you do not depend on another person for your victory. This is a race you run with me only. Your eternal destiny rests in one decision you will make: Will you follow me or not? I have marked out your race for you. I have gone the distance for you and conquered sin and death. I have already won the race. Your victory is secure in me. I stand before you and cheer you on. Run to me, my love. I am your goal. Press on toward your goal and win the prize that God calls you to. Your reward is spending an eternity with my Father and me, in the place to which you have been called. Leave your earthly treasures behind, and gain the riches of an everlasting life in Christ.

"The kingdom of heaven is like treasure hidden in a field. When a man found it, he hid it again, and then in his joy went and sold all he had and bought that field. Again, the kingdom of heaven is like a merchant looking for fine pearls. When he found one of great value, he went away and sold everything he had and bought it." (Matthew 13:44-45)

Be Sold Out for Me

Follow me, my beloved one, and you will find my hidden treasure. Those who do not know me will not inherit my riches. When you discover the gift of my grace, your reward will be life altering. Confess me as your Savior, and the kingdom of heaven belongs to you. Believe that I gave my life for you, and devote yourself to chasing hard after me. Your works are futile, but my grace is enough. You are saved by it. Follow me, and I will reveal my hidden treasure. A life in eternity with me awaits your bidding.

When you decide to follow me, it may cost you all you own; but those who understand the gift of my grace, joyfully pay the price, and sell everything in exchange for the promise of heaven. The meek will inherit the earth. Everlasting life is a gift I place in the hands of the humble. Heaven is the prize that calls you upward to a life with me. Will you place your life in my hands? I have given you everything I have. Will you give me everything you have?

It is difficult for the rich to enter the kingdom of heaven because they have so much to give up. It is easier to give up a little than a lot. When you are blessed with the abundant riches of the world, it is hard to relinquish them. The wealthy do not hold onto their possessions, but their possessions hold on to them. You came into this world with nothing, and you will leave it the same way. Would you trade your earthly possessions for a place in heaven with me?

I have provided the way to everlasting life. If you dig up such a treasure, will you bury it again? The inheritance I offer in the kingdom of heaven far outweighs the value of any riches here on earth. I have sold myself out for you. Will you be sold out for me?

Then, because so many people were coming and going that they did not even have a chance to eat, he said to them, "Come with me by yourselves to a quiet place and get some rest." So they went away by themselves in a boat to a solitary place. (Mark 6:31-32)

A Quiet Place to Rest

My child, you are tired and weary. Come with me to a quiet place and get some rest. Whether you are a busy mom chasing after three children all day, or the executive of a company trying to meet the demands of your subordinates; you need some time of refreshment. Come with me. I will provide a quiet place for you to relax away from the noise of the day. Come with me, and I will fill you up with my love and affection. You will find your respite in me.

I, myself, had to take time away from the crowds and the noise to be refreshed by God, and to restore a renewed spirit within myself. When you feel drained and empty inside with nothing more to give, come to me, and I will recharge you. I will revive your passions. I will energize your strength. I will give you the boost you need to keep going. My support and encouraging words will uplift your soul. I will clear your mind of the clutter, and help you focus on me.

You have my Spirit within you. When you find a quiet place, you will be able to tune in to my voice. My voice will soothe your spirit. I will calm your anxieties. I will quiet you with my love. Find me in the solitude, and experience my peace. How excellent it would be if you started your day this way. Start your engine in my presence every morning. I will invigorate you for the entire day. Call on me throughout your day. I will whisper my words of encouragement to you. Lean on me for your strength, and I will carry you through your difficult situations. Let me refresh you when you have reached your limit. Find me in a quiet place. I will provide rest for your body, peace for your mind, and restoration for your soul.

Still another said, "I will follow you, Lord; but first let me go back and say good-by to my family." Jesus replied, "No one who puts his hand to the plow and looks back is fit for service in the kingdom of God." (Luke 9:61-62)

Don't Look Back

My innocent child, there is a price to pay when you choose to follow me. A disciple's life does not come without a cost. I have no place to lay my head. Not many are willing to travel the path I have chosen. Giving up my family was the cost of doing the will of God, but now the ones who walk with me are my family. Whoever does the will of God and follows me is my family.

When you say you will follow me, do it without conditions. Do not take the time to get your life in order. It is by my grace alone that you are called the sons and daughters of God. You are my family now; you belong to me. There is nothing you can do to prepare for following me. Life, as you once knew it, no longer exists. The dear ones you leave behind will take care of themselves. When I call you, you must get up at once and follow me. There is no time to waste. My kingdom must be proclaimed. Our work is mounting up before our eyes.

Keep your sights in a forward direction. There is no place for hindsight. The things you leave behind are now insignificant. The mission I set before you is much more important; it will bring you great satisfaction. Throw off what hinders you, and fix your eyes on me. I endured the cross for you, and great joy was my reward. How much more joy my Father will reward you with, when you give up everything to follow me.

The one who chases after me, and then looks back, is not ready for service in my kingdom; but I say, do not wait until you are ready. You will never see that day. Come with me now, my child. I will prepare you for that which lies ahead. You have nothing to fear. My perfect love will abolish all your fears. Follow me, and do not look back.

"The bride belongs to the bridegroom. The friend who attends the bridegroom waits and listens for him, and is full of joy when he hears the bridegroom's voice. That joy is mine, and it is now complete." (John 3:29)

The Bride Belongs to the Bridegroom

My church, my bride, you belong to me. You are the one I have come for. I came to collect my bride, and bring her home with me. The wedding celebration cannot begin until the bride and the bridegroom are joined together in holiness. I laid down my life for you. I loved you so much I gave myself up for you to make you holy. You are now without stain or wrinkle, but holy and blameless in my sight. You are a radiant church. Your righteousness shines brighter than the light of one thousand suns. Present yourself to me. It's time to celebrate.

Do you hear me calling you? Does the sound of my voice bring you joy? I am your joy, and your joy is now perfect. Listen to my voice. You know my voice. You hear my whispers. You are my beloved bride. I desire an intimate relationship with you. Will you communicate your heart to me? Will you come to me in the morning? Will you speak with me as you go throughout your day? Will you kneel in prayer beside me in the evening?

I love to spend time with you. I want to hear your concerns. Share your joys as well as your sorrows. I desire a "one flesh" type of relationship with you—where we are so close, we move together, we think alike, and we even complete each other's sentences. My Spirit is joined with your spirit. We are one.

Will you follow me where I lead you? Will you make me the Lord of your life? I have your best interests in mind. I will lead you on paths of righteousness. You are the love of my life. I will honor you and cherish you. I will love you and respect you. I will never leave you or forsake you. I am your faithful bridegroom. I commit myself to you for a lifetime of love and happiness. You will experience my joy, and I will make you complete. You belong to me.

Chapter 3

LISTEN TO ME

*God's Word gives us instructions for everyday
life and relationships.*

The Sovereign Lord has given me an instructed tongue, to know the word that sustains the weary. He wakens me morning by morning, wakens my ear to listen like one being taught. The Sovereign Lord has opened my ears, and I have not been rebellious; I have not drawn back. (Isaiah 50:4-5)

Listen Like One Being Taught

Good morning, my beloved child. Will you listen to my voice today? I will awaken your ears to listen, as I instruct you in my ways. You know the sound of my voice. I will speak to you in a gentle whisper. Do not dismiss my voice. It is I you hear. Do not turn away from what you perceive. In the silence of the morning, your ears are open to my soft voice. Be confident in knowing it is I who address you. Consider the words that fall upon your ears. I do not utter words that are empty. I will disclose the keys to life. Lend your ear to my whispers. Hear my instructions. I will direct your paths.

When you hear from me, it would be best to heed my teachings. My wisdom and knowledge are freely given to you in the expressions I deliver. My wisdom is a priceless treasure. Many search for it, and do not find it, because they do not take the time to listen to my voice; but I have opened your ears. You hear me very clearly. Do you know the value of recognizing my whispers? It is a lost art. Many do not believe that I still speak to my people today. The current times are not unlike the past. My people today do not have faith in me, a *living* God.

Every human being on earth today can hear my voice if they choose to listen. Few will take the initiative to do so. When you make time for me, I will reward your efforts. You will hear my voice clearly. My advice will not fall on deaf ears. Listen to my voice, and pay attention to my instructions. You believe in a living God who wants to direct your ways. Do not turn away from me. Live your life with intentionality and purpose. Understand my desires for you. Be about my work in my kingdom here on earth. Your rewards in heaven will exceed your expectations. In reverence, tune in to my voice each day. Get wisdom, knowledge, and understanding from the one who created you to carry out his will. Listen closely; hear what I have to say to you today. Morning by morning my voice will direct your ways. The instruction on my lips will lead you to an abundant life—the life I have intended for you.

". . . From everyone who has been given much, much will be demanded; and from the one who has been entrusted with much, much more will be asked." *(Luke 12:48b)*

Much Given, Much Required

My trusted one, I have given you much; therefore, I demand as much from you. Do not be stingy with what I have given you. Had I not blessed you with much, what would you have to give? All that you have is a gift from me. I have given you many things. Be willing to share from your wealth. I have given you much wisdom. Pass along what you have learned from me.

I have given you gifts of the Spirit. Do not hoard them, but put them to use. A gift received by the Spirit, and not put to full use, is a wasted gift. If your gift is teaching, the world is your classroom. If your gift is administration, organize the chaos. If your gift is helps, lend your hand. If your gift is giving, give generously. If your gift is prophecy, listen to me before you speak. If your gift is knowledge, know me more intimately. If your gift is speaking in tongues or interpreting tongues, honor me with your gifts. If your gift is shepherding, lead my flock. If your gift is healing, touch the broken. If your gift is faith, move a mountain.

Many gifts I have given—each person receives a different gift, but none of these gifts are worth anything, if you do not have love. I have loved you much. In fact, I have given my life for you. I have given you much. You must be willing to share what you have been given. If you have been loved much, you will be required to love much. Be intentional about loving unselfishly. Love unconditionally. Love unexpectedly. Love never fails. I have entrusted you with much; much more will be required of you. Honor me with your gifts. Give as you have received. Love as you have been loved.

"The fear of the Lord is the beginning of wisdom, and knowledge of the Holy One is understanding." (Proverbs 9:10) My purpose is that they may be encouraged in heart and united in love, so that they may have the full riches of complete understanding, in order that they may know the mystery of God, namely, Christ, in whom are hidden all the treasures of wisdom and knowledge. (Colossians 2:2-3)

Wisdom is Supreme

Knowledge brings understanding, and understanding brings wisdom. Gain knowledge of me, and understanding will follow. Turn your ear to my wisdom, and apply your heart to understanding. Listen to my instruction, and you will understand my ways. By wisdom I laid the earth's foundations; by understanding I set the heavens in place. Look for it as silver; search for it as hidden treasure. Then you will understand the fear of the Lord, and find the knowledge of God. I give wisdom; from my mouth come knowledge and understanding.

Search for me, my child. Look for me as for hidden treasure. I hold riches in my right hand; I am just waiting to give them to you. Fear me in reverence, and surely, my wisdom will be yours. Do not forget my words or swerve from them. Wisdom is supreme; therefore, get wisdom. It may cost you everything, but find understanding. I guide you in the way of wisdom. Hold on to my instruction.

Time with me is well spent. Make time to listen to my voice. My voice will guide you, and lead you along straight paths. Ask for my wisdom; my wisdom will I give you. Know me; discover my ways, and understanding will follow. Listen to me, and you will live in safety. Be at ease, without fear of harm. Keep my commands in your heart; your life will be long and prosperous. Preserve sound judgment and discernment; they will be life for you. When you lie down, have no fear. Your sleep will be sweet. I will be your confidence, and I will keep your foot from the snares of life. Seek me alone for wisdom; my wisdom is supreme.

"But I tell you who hear me: Love your enemies, do good to those who hate you, bless those who curse you, pray for those who mistreat you." (Luke 6:27-28)

Love Your Enemies

My darling, you hear me correctly. Love your enemies. Yes, I say love them, pray for them, bless them, do good things to them. When you do good things to your human opponents, your spiritual enemy, the devil, has no basis for attack. In loving your human enemy, she has no reason to hate you. When you bless her, her heart softens in my hand. Pray for her, and I will intercede for her. When you do these things, the anger and resentment you hold onto will fade away. As the bitterness fades away, loving your enemies will become easier.

See your adversary through my eyes. She is my child, too. I created her, just as I created you. The challenges that molded her in life may be different than your challenges. She has been wounded by her own enemies. Her heart has hardened in her own self-defense. Her responses to her ordeals may not be honoring to me, but examine your own heart. Are you without fault?

As you pray for her, set your mind on the things above. You cannot do this in your own strength, but I am with you. When you do not have the words to pray, I will step in and help you. The one you oppose is my child too. Would you be the one to bring her back to me? Would your actions be honoring to me? Do you think more of me than you do of yourself? Listen to my commands. Obey my teaching. Honor me with your ways. Pray for your adversary, and bless her through me. When you go against your own nature and love your enemies, your rewards will be great, both internally and eternally. Reap the benefits of my love when you love each other unconditionally as I have loved you.

See, I have engraved you on the palms of my hands; your walls are ever before me. (Isaiah 49:16)

On the Palms of My Hands

My precious child, you are struggling in your relationship with your sister because you do not see eye to eye. You and your sister are two different people. I designed you that way. Do you understand how boring life would be if all human beings were created from the same mold? Celebrate your differences. You are both my children. You are both created in my own image. The fact that you are different should not mean that you cannot enjoy each other.

In your sister, you may see and understand another facet of my character. Find the good in her and concentrate on that alone. Accept your differences, and learn to live side-by-side with your sister. Remember, I created her, but life has also shaped her into the woman she has become. You may not know or understand the trials she has faced, but they have carved out her character as much as I have. She is who she is because of what she has lived.

You know the same is true for you. You are not only the person I designed and created; you are the riverbed that has been carved out by the rushing waters of time. Some of your design is straight from my hand, and some has been formed by the paths you have chosen; but I use it all for your good. Nothing sifts through my hand, but what I have already approved for you.

Do not be distracted by what you see on the outside. Look deeper within your sister and you will see a reflection of me. Be a friend to the person within. You know all women are mysterious, as I am. Dig deeper, and celebrate the part of her that I have authored. I have engraved you both on the palms of my hands. I have called you both by name. You are mine.

Wives, submit to your husbands as to the Lord. For the husband is the head of the wife as Christ is the head of the church, his body, of which he is the Savior. Now as the church submits to Christ, so also wives should submit to their husbands in everything . . . . However, each one of you must love his wife as he loves himself, and the wife must respect her husband. (Ephesians 5:22-24, 33)

Do You Respect Me?

My precious daughter, do you find it difficult and challenging to respect your own husband? You are not alone. Many women resist this challenge. For me it is simple. Do you respect me? Do you love me? If you say that you do, you must obey my commands. I have created men to feel loved by feeling respected. Men respect other men much more easily than women respect men.

A woman does not always understand that love and respect are one in the same for a man. A woman does not feel loved by being respected, as a man feels loved. A woman feels loved when a man is willing to lay down his life for her, as I have done for my bride, the church. That is not to say that a man will be a woman's servant or that a woman will be a man's servant, but I have commanded you to serve one another in love. A man shows his love for his wife by providing for her and protecting her. He gives himself up for her by setting aside his own desires and putting her desires above his own.

I did not say that a wife should respect her husband when he deserves it. Respect is as unconditional as love. A woman must respect her husband whether he has earned it or not. A man must love his wife whether she deserves it or not. I have laid out the chain of command for you. Wives submit to your husbands as to the Lord, husbands submit to me. When you do not submit to your husband or respect your husband, you do not submit to me or respect me. You do as you should do, and let me worry about your husband's actions. You are accountable to your husband. He is accountable to me. Respect him, and you respect me. Deny him, and you deny me. Love him, and you love me. Do you respect me?

". . . For I know the plans I have for you," declares the Lord, "plans to prosper you and not to harm you, plans to give you hope and a future. Then you will call upon me and come and pray to me, and I will listen to you. You will seek me and find me when you seek me with all your heart. I will be found by you," declares the Lord. (Jeremiah 29:11-14a)

Call Upon Me

Good morning, my child. As a mother, you cannot believe that your daughter is all grown up? She wants help making a decision, a direction in her life choices? You are asking me for help on advising her? Time passes very quickly. Not too long ago you were her age—ready to go out on your own in the world. I could give you an answer for her. I could instruct you on what she should do, but this time, I think you should encourage your daughter to seek me as you do. Teach her how to pursue me. Train her how to hear and recognize my voice. This is a turning point. Rather than getting advice and answers from you, she will learn to come to me. We would be so much further ahead if someone had taught you to seek me in this way at her age.

Your role with your daughter is changing, my love. It will be difficult to relinquish that position of control in her life, but it is time. It is time for you to usher her into my presence. Take her hand, and lead her to me. She already knows me. I am not a stranger to her, but my relationship with her has not developed into this yet. I do not hear from her or connect with her like this. If you were to suggest this to her, and she were to try it, I would surely make myself known to her.

Once she connects with me in this way, she will be set for life. She can seek me wherever life takes her. She will be all the richer when she learns to speak to me and listen for my voice. You know I have a plan for her, a plan to prosper her and not to harm her, a plan to give her hope and a future. When she calls on me, I will listen. When she seeks me with all of her heart, she will find me. Train her to seek me; I will answer her. I will be waiting.

Because of the Lord's great love we are not consumed, for his compassions never fail. They are new every morning; great is your faithfulness. I say to myself, "The Lord is my portion; therefore I will wait for him." The Lord is good to those whose hope is in him, to the one who seeks him; it is good to wait quietly for the salvation of the Lord. (Lamentations 3:22-26)

Wait Quietly

You come to me today because you have been disappointed again by the one you love. In your anger and hurt, you seek me asking me to change your offender. You have been faithful in your daily prayers for a spiritual makeover. You wonder why your dedication has not been rewarded—why your devoted prayers have not been answered by me yet. You want to see a transformation take place in your timeframe and in your lifetime.

My dear sweet child, reach a little deeper and conjure up some more patience. Love is patient. Be patient with me; be patient with him. I do not force myself on anyone. I will do my work when he is ready. That has not happened yet. What should you do until then? Love him; respect him. Be Jesus to him. Be a model of my love for him. Do not give in to your human ways, but seek me for the strength to love him and respect him unconditionally. Without me in your life, these things are not possible in your own power.

Stay close to me, and watch how I love him. I love him and forgive him no matter what he does. You must do the same. Forgive him, and then forgive him again and again. When you forgive him, you must also forget as I do. Each day is a new day. Each day I give you a clean slate to start with; you must do the same for him. He will continue to disappoint you. You must be consistent with your love no matter what he does. Love is not always a feeling. Love is a commitment. Love him even when you do not feel like it. Love him even when he does not deserve it. Love him at all times. Remember that he feels loved by being respected. Whenever I say love, you know I also mean respect. Remember to put your hope and trust in me. Seek me, and then wait quietly for me to do my work. You do your part; I'll do mine.

"A new command I give you: Love one another. As I have loved you, so you must love one another. All men will know that you are my disciples if you love one another." (John 13:34-35)

Love One Another

Love isn't love until you give it away. Be free with your love. Turn to another, and love him or her as I have loved you. Love your friend sacrificially. To love someone well, you must lay down your life for the other. You must be willing to set aside your own desires, and devote yourself to another. Love is not always a feeling, but is more of a commitment. Love one another, even when you don't feel like it. Love one another, because I have loved you first. Take my love and offer it to the one who seems unlovable. Love him or her anyway.

This is love. I left my throne in heaven to walk on earth in the flesh. I was despised and rejected by men as was prophesied of old. I suffered criticism and torture to carry out my Father's will. I was sentenced to death on a cross; I was pierced for your transgressions. I laid down my own life in exchange for your freedom. My death has cleared your name. You have been set free from the wages of your sin, by my death. You are now reconciled to my Father, by my act of love. I have loved you sacrificially.

First, love the Lord your God with all your heart, soul, mind, and strength; then love each other as you have been loved by me. Walk with your friend through tough times. Love your neighbor as you love yourself. Love the one who has been rejected. Love your enemies, and do good things to those who hate you. Love your spouse as I have loved my bride, the church. Give up your own desires to fulfill this law of love.

When you love each other in the same manner I have loved you, the world sees me in you. The world will know me by watching you love in this way. It will be evident to those around you that you are my disciple. If you love me, you will obey me. Let others see me in you by loving another with my kind of love. Be a strong witness for me. Love one another.

"Honor your father and your mother, as the Lord your God has commanded you, so that you may live long and that it may go well with you in the land the Lord your God is giving you." (Deuteronomy 5:16)

Honor Dad and Mom

Obey my commands. When you do, I promise you things will go well for you, and you may enjoy a long life on the earth. I have said, "Children obey your parents." This is what I ask of you. You may think this command applies to young children only, but as you mature in life, the "obey" becomes more of a reverence and respect for your parents. Out of respect for your parents, you will choose to act upon their advice, abide by their rules, comply with their wishes, and follow through with their requests. It sounds a lot like obeying, doesn't it?

Respect for your parent, as much as love, should not be conditional. It is something I ask you to do whether or not your parent deserves the respect. When you respect your parents unconditionally, I have promised you a long, thriving life.

Your father may have disappointed you in the past. Your mother may upset you at times. Your parents may not be the people you wish they would be. They have made mistakes; they are not perfect, but still, they are the parents I have chosen for you. Do not dishonor your father and your mother. Forgiveness is yours to give freely; whether they ask for it or not. Forgive them as I have forgiven you.

You may be the first person who has loved and respected your father or your mother. There may be no one else on earth that has chosen to regard them highly. Your parents have made sacrifices for you. Your parents have given you life. What you do with that life is up to you now. Your parents raised you to the best of their ability. In some cases, that may not seem like enough. No matter how they have messed up at times, I am asking you to honor them. Respect your parents, and you will have honored them and me with your life.

"'For this reason a man will leave his father and mother and be united to his wife, and the two will become one flesh.' So they are no longer two, but one."
(Mark 10:7-8)

Not Two, But One

One flesh, one mind, one heart, one spirit—the two will become one. The husband and wife that I have joined together; let no one and nothing separate them. Before you were married, you were an individual person. You thought of yourself. You took care of yourself. You fed yourself and clothed yourself. You had only one person to look after. Now that you and your spouse have been united in marriage, you have another person to take care of, as you would your own body.

Care for your mate, as you would care for yourself. Love your husband, as you would love yourself. Wives submit yourselves to your husbands, as you would submit yourself to the authority of Christ. Respect your husband, as you respect the Lord Jesus. Husbands love your wives, as you love your own body. Love your wives, as Christ loved his bride, the church. Be willing to lay down your life for your spouse. Put the other person ahead of yourself.

I am the one who created you, and gave you the breath of life. I have numbered your days, and called you by name. I have made your body my temple, my dwelling place. My Spirit who lives inside you has become one with your spirit. Remember me, and put me in first place in your life. Enjoy the intimacy of a close relationship with me, by connecting to my Holy Spirit. You are my bride. I have become one with you. I have made you a priority in my life. I love to communicate with you. I know your most secret thoughts. I know you better than you know yourself.

After me, your spouse is your second highest priority. You may experience the same kind of oneness that you and I enjoy. You may communicate your deepest longings to your mate. In fact, that is the kind of relationship that I intended for you. In sharing your private desires with your husband, he will be better able to meet your needs and wants. He will know you and care for you as I do. He will set aside his own desires to fulfill your expectations. He will more fully understand your inner workings. When you are honest with yourself and him, through open communication, your hearts will become one.

Your spirit, together with mine, will join his spirit and become one spirit. With my Holy Spirit in the center of your lives, everything else becomes more unified. We will all work together and run like a finely tuned engine. One can anticipate the other's thoughts and actions, but keep open the communication; without it, nothing good will be accomplished.

Saturate your minds with my Word. Be like-minded in Christ. When you seek to be transformed by the renewing of your minds, you will become more like Christ Jesus. As your minds are made new for Jesus, you will see eye-to-eye on the important things of life. Your thoughts and desires will be in harmony with my will. Our minds will be of one accord.

It seems that one flesh is most obviously achieved through your sexual union, but that is not the only reason or means to become one flesh. In caring for your own body, you demonstrate your love for your spouse. You would not neglect your own body; do not neglect your spouse. The flesh is the surface that holds everything else in place. When you achieve oneness in heart, mind, and spirit, these components will be held together by becoming one flesh.

When all of these aspects achieve unity, the result is spiritual harmony. Three cords intertwined together are stronger than one alone. Strengthen your relationship by being intertwined with each other and with my Spirit. I am the glue that binds you together for all of time. Nothing will separate what I have joined together. Seek me, find me, and live in me, as I am living in you.

". . . I prayed for this child, and the Lord has granted me what I asked of him. So now I give him to the Lord. For his whole life he will be given over to the Lord." And he worshiped the Lord there. (1 Samuel 1:27-28)

Surrender

What I entrusted to you many years ago never belonged to you in the first place. The children I blessed you with were not yours to relinquish. From the beginning, the children I created in your womb were my own. I gave them life, and placed them in your care for a season of your life and theirs. You got them through bottles, diapers, and preschool in their early childhood days. You taught them about me. You trained them in my ways. As they grew, you taught them to be independent. You modeled your love and devotion to me. They learned to depend on me, knowing I will provide for their every need.

Now the time has come for you to send them off. All the days of their young lives, this is what you have prepared them for, to live apart from you. You have done your best to raise them to know me, love me, and obey me. You have taught them the ways of the world, and protected them from the dangers that lurk outside the walls of your home.

You have taught them to seek my wisdom and discernment for all things. They are bright children, good students, and fine leaders in their own sphere of influence. It may seem to you that they will not be able to manage things on their own, without your help; but you will find that I will make provision for them. Surrender your children to me. This means you will turn them over to my care and protection. Relinquish the supposed control you had assumed for them, and allow me to lead them down the paths I have chosen and prepared for them. I plan to prosper them.

Hope in me, and trust me to take over from here. I have always been involved in their rearing, but now my role as their coach, body guard, teacher, savior, and friend will stand above any role you may feel you play in their existence. As they mature into fully functioning adults, the control you once had over their lives will dissipate before your very eyes. Your knowledge of their hour-by-hour and day-to-day activities will come to a screeching halt, but my eyes are forever upon them. I see everything they do. I know every move they make. I will watch over them and protect them from harm.

See the lilies of the field. They neither toil nor spin, but I provide for them. How much more will I provide for you and for your offspring. I have good gifts yet to give them. My blessings are one hundred fold. My favor is upon them. Place your children in my arms, and leave the rest to me. No worry of yours is justified. Do not cling to that which does not belong to you. You have done your job; the balance is in my hands. I am more than capable to produce good fruit in their lives. Surrender your dear ones to me. I am in control. My will prevails in the hearts of those who love me and call me their Lord.

Blessed is the man who finds wisdom, the man who gains understanding, for she is more profitable than silver and yields better returns than gold. She is more precious than rubies; nothing you desire can compare with her. Long life is in her right hand; in her left are riches and honor. Her ways are pleasant ways, and all her paths are peace. She is a tree of life to those who embrace her; those who lay hold of her will be blessed. (Proverbs 3:13-18)

Blessed with Wisdom

Arise, my precious one; you are blessed. Wisdom, understanding, and insight are as a hidden treasure. Search high and low to find them. Wisdom is mine to give you. Knowledge and understanding flow from my lips. When you find wisdom, longevity of life with riches and honor are yours for the taking. Trust in me. Do not be wise in your own ways. Acknowledge me, and I will lead you down respectable paths.

In keeping with love and faithfulness, you will win favor in my eyes. I will be your confidence and your strength for the journey. Reverence to me is the establishment of your wisdom and understanding. Do not give into sin. Listen to me, and I will make my thoughts known to you. Revere me, and live in the safety I will provide you. Fear no evil. I am with you.

Wisdom is the ultimate gift. Grace and brilliance will be your crowning glory. Listen to me. My words are life to your soul and health to your body. Do not swerve to the left or to the right, but remain upright and pursue the straight path. Guard your heart. Fix your eyes upon me. Do not be quick to walk in the ways of the wicked. Shun evil, and go your own way.

My wisdom is more valuable than precious gems, silver, and gold. I will bestow wealth on those who love me. Rejoice in me, and I will give you sound judgment. I have delighted in you since the day I first conceived you in my mind. Nothing would please me more than to receive your love and devotion in return. Honor me with your first fruits. Remain humble in my sight. When you seek me, you will find life. Find wisdom, and your days will be many.

Devote yourselves to prayer, being watchful and thankful. (Colossians 4:2)

Pray

My child, your prayers are of great worth to me. Be steadfast in prayer, and stay on the straight path which leads to my heart. When you pray, I listen. Your words are not empty. They do not go unnoticed. Give yourself over to prayer, and stay close to me. Dedicate your thoughts to me. Offer me your adoration, and I will provide for all your needs. I know what you need before you ask. Devote yourself to prayer. Pray continuously, on all occasions, with all kinds of requests. Make your requests known to me, and I will lavish my grace upon you like a crown of garland around your head.

Be watchful. Pay close attention to me. Be expectant. Your prayers will be answered. In my time and in my way, my answer will come to you. It may be exactly what you ask for, or it may be exactly what you need. The two are not always the same. My ways are higher than your ways. I know the future. I see what is best for you. I answer your prayers according to my perfect plan. You may not know or understand my will, but my ways are perfect. Be ready to receive all that I have to give you. Anticipate the blessings you will receive when you pray in Jesus' name according to my perfect will.

Give thanks for everything in all circumstances. Every good gift is from above. Give thanks when it is easy to see my work in your life. Give thanks when you do not see my work at all. Give thanks for each day that you take a breath. Give thanks for every pleasure on this earth. Give thanks in the midst of your trials. My hand is upon you in all seasons of your life. Appreciate all things, big and small. The little things in life are some of my greatest gifts. Be joyful in all situations. Delight yourself in me. The desires of your heart, I will give you. Your face is radiant when you submit yourself to me in prayer. I look upon you. I enjoy what I see.

I know what it is to be in need, and I know what it is to have plenty. I have learned the secret of being content in any and every situation, whether well fed or hungry, whether living in plenty or in want. I can do everything through him who gives me strength. (Philippians 4:12-13)

Be Content

The secret of contentment lies in your relationship with me. You can do all things through me. You will find satisfaction when you belong to me. Whether you live in the biggest house on the block or reside in a one room shed, your happiness does not depend on the material items you possess. Be pleased with what you hold in your hand. Do not look to the future and think, "If only I had this or that, I would be happy." Receiving everything you desire will not set you at ease.

Your unhappiness is not a result of your lack of wealth. Rather, your wealth is the result of your unhappiness. You are driven by your desire for bigger, better, more. You give up your freedom when you are controlled by greed. You work long hours, sacrificing time with your loved ones, to afford the objects of your desire. As you sign on the dotted line of credit, you relinquish any time you would have to enjoy the item you just purchased.

My Son had no place to lay his head, he had no home to call his own, yet he was King of kings and Lord of lords. Do not spend your life working to pay for the riches the world would have you own, but spend your days doing the work of your Father in heaven. Enjoy the treasures a life in Christ will afford you. Rely on the one who created you to love you. Bask in the assurance of spiritual prosperity as you seek to know your Creator. Be content with being the child of the King. Live abundantly in the promise of spending your eternity with the God of the universe. Enjoy the life I have placed you in. Do not strive to achieve the life I have not designed for you to have. Be content in me.

"Therefore I tell you, whatever you ask for in prayer, believe that you have received it, and it will be yours. And when you stand praying, if you hold anything against anyone, forgive him, so that your Father in heaven may forgive you your sins." (Mark 11:24-25)

No Room for Resentment

My beloved one, come to me in prayer. I love to hear you present your requests before me. How is your faith? Do you believe I will give you what you ask for? Pray it, believe it, and receive it. Ask for anything in my name, believe it, and it will be yours; but if you pray while you hold on to resentment toward a brother or sister, your words will return empty. Do not conceal your bitterness. Do not harbor a grudge against anyone. Forgive the trespasses that offended you, so that I may forgive your trespasses that offend me.

This is not a request. I instruct you out of the greatness of my heart. Your spiritual health is my first priority. Our relationship has to remain pure, unscathed by the sin of an unforgiving heart. You must forgive because you, yourself, have been forgiven. I bore the guilt of your sin. I died in your place. You will not suffer the sting of the death penalty. You have been excused from your sentence and reconciled to your Creator. I have pardoned your offenses.

You have been given the gift of new life, even life eternal. Extend the same grace to another—the forgiveness that I have extended to you. Holding onto resentment causes the most harm to the owner of it. Forgive your offender, and experience the freedom of letting go. It takes more effort to hold onto a grudge than it does to release it, but more importantly, my hands will not be tied by the power of your resentment. Sin causes a separation from me that I despise. Please check your unforgiving spirit at the door. Do not approach me until you have been reconciled to your brother. I will be waiting for you with great anticipation. I can't wait to be with you again. Listen to my instructions, and remove any obstacles between us. You'll be amazed at how good it feels. The possibilities are limitless. The feeling of freedom is worth the risk of letting go.

For this reason a man will leave his father and mother and be united to his wife, and they will become one flesh. (Genesis 2:24)

The Two Shall Become One

As husband and wife, God joins two individuals, and they become one flesh. Marriage is modeled after the relationship of the Holy Trinity. We are three individuals, God, Jesus, and the Holy Spirit, who are joined in a perfect harmonious relationship called the Trinity. Each one of us is God. We are equal to each other, yet the three of us joined together become one. One, plus one, plus one, equals one. Don't spend too much time trying to figure it all out—it's my kind of math.

In marriage, a man and woman, who are equal to each other, are joined together to become one flesh. It is God's design that the two he created as individuals will live together united and in harmony. In order to live together, in harmony, like the Trinity; God has designed the marriage relationship to be like the relationship between God and myself, and myself and my bride (the church). God is the head of Christ, and Christ is the head of his bride (the church), and man is the head of woman.

As God, Jesus, and the Holy Spirit are equal individuals in the Trinity, man and woman are equal individuals in the marriage relationship. Even though they are equal, Jesus and the Holy Spirit willingly submit themselves to God as the head of their union. Just as I submit myself to God, wives should submit to their husbands as to the Lord. As the church submits to Christ, wives should submit to their husbands in everything.

I, Christ, am equal to God, yet I submitted myself to God's plan of salvation. I willingly and obediently gave my life on the cross, in exchange for yours, so that God's will would be carried out. So too, wives, though equal to their husbands, should submit themselves to the direction and leadership of their husband; but still I say, all believers must submit themselves one to another. Husbands must love their wives, as I love the church. A man should be willing to set aside his own desires, and lay down his life for his bride. A man must love and care for his wife as he does his own body. A man would not neglect his own body and neither should he neglect his wife.

When a man and woman become one, they reflect the relationship of the Trinity. To be like the Trinity, each one should be like and act like Jesus Christ. You must be concerned that all you do will bring glory to God. Humble yourself, and submit yourself to the will of God. Set aside your own desires, and make your purpose in life to live as Christ, and bring glory to God, the Father.

I would not ask you to do anything I have not already done myself. I submit myself to the headship of God, and I ask wives to submit themselves to the leadership of their husbands. Not because you are not worthy or not equal, but because this is God's design and will for marriage. By submitting yourself to your husband, you are submitting yourself to God. God is glorified when his people serve him, obey him, and carry out *his* instructions.

What a privilege it is to be in a marriage relationship with another and experience the intimacy, unity, and harmony that imitate the relationship of the Holy Trinity. Give yourselves to one another, as Christ gave himself to the church. Love each other sacrificially and unconditionally. Submit yourselves to one another and to God. What God joins together in holy matrimony, let no one and nothing destroy. Husbands, be one with your wives. Wives, be one with your husbands. This is all made possible through Christ.

The end of a matter is better than its beginning, and patience is better than pride. Do not be quickly provoked in your spirit, for anger resides in the lap of fools. (Ecclesiastes 7:8-9)

Patience before Pride

When you find yourself in a difficult situation; be patient and see it through. The end of the matter will always be better than the start, if only because it's the end. Do not let a spirit of anger rise up within you. Anger may cause a person to sin. Rather be tolerant of the situation, and endure it without grumbling and complaining. Patient endurance produces character. The patient will inherit the promises of God.

Do not be arrogant in times of difficulty, but in humility, consider others better than yourself. Do not hold onto your pride, it will surely lead to destruction. Patiently wait upon the Lord. Serve him in good times and bad. Be patient in hope, it will be an anchor for your soul, and get you through the long days before you.

Put your faith and trust in me alone. I am in control of all things, and have my best in mind for you. My time table is different from yours. My days seem like years to you, and my hours seem like weeks. Before you realize it, you will have reached the end of the suffering. Approach each matter with patience, and in the end, you will be rewarded.

Patient perseverance produces moral fiber. Practicing patience is a step in your sanctification process. As you practice patience, you become more and more like Christ. Subject yourself to the Spirit of God within you, and I, myself, will sanctify you through and through. You are not your own. You have been sanctified in Christ. Through his death, you are reconciled to me.

Be patient in your suffering. I will see you through. When you have reached the end, you will look back and say, "With God's help I made it through." Now claim the promises I give you. Your inheritance unfolds before you—a life of eternity with me in heaven.

Love must be sincere. Hate what is evil; cling to what is good. Be devoted to one another in brotherly love. Honor one another above yourselves. (Romans 12:9-10)

Be Devoted to One Another

My dearest child, be sincere with your love. The evil one would jump at the chance to taint the good things in your life, such as love. Do not entertain the schemes of the devil. When you love someone, genuinely love them. Be honest and truthful with your love. Do not hold your love over them as a means of control. Do not play games with love. Love is a gift from me, and it should be taken seriously. Cling to all that is good; hate the forces of evil.

Love is faithful. Do not be disloyal in your love. Love may start as an emotion or a feeling, but when feelings fade as time passes, commitment is at the core of true love. Be devoted to one another in love. Consider others better than yourself. The purest kind of love is sacrificial love. Jesus' love for you was purely sacrificial love. To love as Jesus loved, you must be willing to lay down your life for your friend.

Respect the ones you love. Esteem them highly. Hold them at a place above yourself. Regard highly those you love and those who love you. Value one another as buried treasure. Be true to your own heart. Do not lead another on with the premise of love, but follow through on my command to love each other. You must love one another because I loved you first. My love was not meant for you to keep to yourself. I intended for my love to be shared friend to friend, brother to brother, husband to wife, parent to child, among all peoples of the earth. Devote yourselves to loving each other.

Do not turn your back and run from love. Love binds all things together. Be bound by love, in love, for love's sake. Resist the lies of the evil one, and cling to the truth. Love is by far the most excellent way. Love does not fail. It is not self-seeking and does not remember mistakes. Love fills the emptiness of a lonely heart. It gives way to an unlovable spirit.

Therefore, as God's chosen people, holy and dearly loved, clothe yourselves with compassion, kindness, humility, gentleness and patience. Bear with each other and forgive whatever grievances you may have against one another. Forgive as the Lord forgave you. And over all these virtues put on love, which binds them all together in perfect unity. (Colossians 3:12-14)

Forgive as the Lord Forgave You

You are one of my chosen people. I have set you apart. When you confessed me as your Savior, you died to your former ways. You were crucified with me. You live no more, but I live in you. Put to death any of your old earthly ways like: anger, rage, malice, filthy language, and lies. Put on your new self, which is being renewed in the image of your Creator. Therefore, be kind, compassionate, humble, gentle, and patient. This is the manner in which I lived while I was on the earth.

Live as one who is holy because you belong to me. Be tolerant of each other, and forgive each other in all things. Forgive as you have been forgiven. Your Father in heaven does not hold anything against you. When you confess your sin, God forgives you without question. Your Father in heaven does not keep a record of wrongs. You must do the same. When you forgive someone, forget their misdeeds. Remember them no more. God, in his ultimate grace and mercy, has provided the way to forgiveness. If you forgive others of their sins, God will forgive you of yours; but if you do not forgive others of their sins, God will not forgive yours.

Above all things practice my love. This is the most desirable quality you have to give. Love will forgive a multitude of sins. Love binds all these things together in harmony. Do not love as the world does. Practice my love. Love does not fail. It is the most excellent way. If you have all these good features, and do not display my love, you are just making a loud noise. You have gained nothing; but when you put on my love to love another person, they will experience God himself through his image bearer. Love as you have been loved. Forgive as the Lord forgave you.

Your attitude should be the same as that of Christ Jesus: Who, being in very nature God, did not consider equality with God something to be grasped, but made himself nothing, taking the very nature of a servant, being made in human likeness. And being found in appearance as a man, he humbled himself and became obedient to death—even death on a cross! (Philippians 2:5-8)

The Nature of a Servant

It is the mystery that very few understand—fully God and fully man. I am by nature God, but took on the nature of a servant. I humbled myself, in order to be obedient to God. I submitted myself to the authority of the Father, to carry out his amazing plan of salvation. I left my throne in heaven, to live and walk the earth in the form of a man. For the joy set before me, I endured the shame and humility of death on a cross. Understanding that obedience gives way to joy, I willingly died for your sins. Then God exalted me to the highest place, and gave me authority over everything in heaven and on earth and under the earth.

Will you be of one mind with me? Complete my joy by being like-minded. My Spirit lives in you. You have the mind of Christ within you. We are one in spirit and purpose. Align yourself with the Spirit, and do the will of your Father in heaven. Humble yourself, taking on the nature of a servant. Your obedience will bring you joy and glorify your Father in heaven.

I did not come to earth to be served, but to serve others by giving my life as payment for the lives of many. To become great in the kingdom of heaven, you must first be a servant here on earth. Humble yourself before the Lord, and you will be crowned with salvation, and lifted up for all of eternity. Be submissive to the authority of God, and you will be exalted. Be gentle and humble in heart, and you will be the recipient of God's grace, mercy, and peace.

Serve one another with the love of Christ in your heart. Uphold the law I established, and love your neighbor as yourself. The most important thing is faith expressed through love. Plant the seed that pleases the Spirit, and collect eternal life from the Spirit. Let us do good things to all people, especially your fellow believers. Practice the nature of a servant.

Chapter 4

TRUST IN ME

*We relinquish our control to God
who protects us and prospers us.*

Trust in the Lord with all your heart and lean not not on your own understanding; in all your ways acknowledge him and he will make your paths straight. (Proverbs 3:5-6)

Trust in Me

My child, the most valuable lessons are learned in "the process." That is true with everything. If I made this all happen for you in a moment, what would you learn from that? You know I can do anything. I can make it happen tomorrow if I choose. There is much for you to know yet. Your growth is part of this process. I may choose to expedite some steps in the process, but you will still experience "the process."

Here is the lesson for now—*trust me.* "Trust in me with all your heart and lean not on your own understanding. In all your ways acknowledge me and I will make your paths straight." (Proverbs 3:5-6) This is a verse for a lifetime; now live it. Let me break it down for you.

You need to "trust me."

You need to "trust me with all."

You need to "trust me with all your heart."

You need to "lean."

You need to "lean not on your own."

You need to "lean not on your own understanding."

You need to "acknowledge."

You need to "acknowledge me."

You need to "acknowledge me in all."

You need to "acknowledge me in all your ways."

You need to "acknowledge me in all your ways and I will."

You need to "acknowledge me in all your ways and I will make your paths."

You need to "acknowledge me in all your ways and I will make your paths straight."

You need to "trust in me with all your heart and lean not on your own understanding; in all your ways acknowledge me and I will make your paths straight."

You need to.

You need.

You

Understand? It's up to you. It's up to you to trust me. I am in control. I will not fail you. I will make your paths straight. The shortest distance between two points is a straight line. Trust in me, and I will make your paths straight; it will be the shortest distance for you to travel in "the process."

Then the Lord said to Moses, "I will rain down bread from heaven for you. The people are to go out each day and gather enough for that day. In this way I will test them and see whether they will follow my instructions. On the sixth day they are to prepare what they bring in, and that is to be twice as much as they gather on the other days." (Exodus 16:4-5)

Manna for Today

My beloved one, you know this story well. I had just freed my people from hundreds of years of bondage with Pharaoh, and all they could do was grumble and complain. They did not trust me, the God who released them from slavery, to take care of their needs. It wasn't so much that I wouldn't allow them to gather bread for several days; it was a test to see if they would follow my instructions. They needed to remember that I was in control, and that they could depend on me.

Many of them did not follow my instructions. They took more bread than they needed for the day, and the leftovers were rotten by the next morning. Or they did not gather two days' worth before the Sabbath, and went out on the Sabbath to gather manna, but they found none. To trust me is to depend on me completely. Have confidence that I will do what I say I will do. I will provide.

Each day brings enough trouble of its own. You need not worry about tomorrow. Leave that to me. Can you trust me that completely? Have you put all your faith and hope in me? When you do, I will rain down bread from heaven, enough to satisfy you each day, and you will never go hungry again. Gather the manna you need for today, and rely on me for tomorrow.

Train a child in the way he should go, and when he is old he will not turn from it. (Proverbs 22:6)

Let Go and Let Me

My child, I am sympathetic with your struggles. To sit back and watch your adult child make his or her own way through life, without willingly accepting your guidance, is no easy task. To give up control in one's life is understandably difficult. I know. May I remind you that I am in control of all things? I always have been. Whether you admit to it or accept it, I am in control. As you come to grips with your feelings of uncertainty, know that I am not uncertain. As you relinquish your hypothetical feeling of control in your child's life, know that I AM. As you relate to how I feel when you trudge off on your own, without seeking me first, you will understand my ways more completely.

I will never leave you or forsake you. Your child was my child first. I have never lost sight of him. I never will. I will protect him from harm. I will guide his ways when he asks. I will allow him to choose his path—just as I allowed you to choose yours. He will not use good judgment at times. He will make mistakes. He will lose his way. Remember when you did the same? Most children do not learn from their parents' mistakes. He is no different, but he was my child first.

You have done the best you can with him. Now you will have to release him to me completely. Let go and let me. I am able. I am capable. I know what is best for him. You have raised him to know me. His foundation has been set on me, the Rock. You have trained him in the way he should go, and when he is old he will not turn from it. He may lose his way now and then, but he will find his way back home to you—to me. Trust me. Depend on me. Have faith in me. I will not fail you.

There is no fear in love. But perfect love drives out fear, because fear has to do with punishment. The man who fears is not made perfect in love. (1 John 4:18) "Peace I leave with you; my peace I give you. I do not give to you as the world gives. Do not let your hearts be troubled and do not be afraid." (John 14:27)

Be Not Afraid

My child, do not be afraid of what will be. Your life is too short to spend a moment entertaining anxious thoughts about what tomorrow will bring. Cast all your cares and burdens upon me. Let me worry about tomorrow. I will bear your burdens. I will carry you because I love you. I have loved you with an everlasting love. My love is perfect. Were you to understand the depth of my love for you, worry would no longer remain in your heart.

Consider this: I laid down my life for you. I stood in the gap for a fallen world. There is no greater love than this. My perfect love drives out your fear. You must know me better, to understand me better. Spend time with me to know me. I am love. I am patient and kind. I am not easily angered. I do not keep a record of your wrongs. I will protect you. I will not fail you. I am here for you. Allow me to love you out of your fear.

Will you accept the peace I have to give you? I do not give to you as the world gives. My love is not conditional. I love you no matter what. There is nothing you can do to make me love you more. There is nothing you can do to make me love you less. My love for you is constant and unconditional. My love is the most excellent gift I have to give you. Without my love, you are nothing. When you know me and understand me, you will accept my love for its worth. My love is sufficient for you. I am all you need. Cast me not away. Draw near to me, and I will draw near to you. Let me love you, and do not be afraid.

Accept the peace I give you. It's not like anything you have ever experienced. It will surpass everything you currently understand about peace. You will have no worries believing that I am in control and trusting me for everything. Nothing will clutter your mind and heart.

Though he brings grief, he will show compassion, so great is his unfailing love. For he does not willingly bring affliction or grief to the children of men. (Lamentations 3:32-33)

Perfect Love

Child of sorrow, lift up your head. The sun is shining in the eastern sky. Brighter days await you. I have not willingly brought this affliction upon you. Your grief is reasonable, but my compassion will erase your tears. My perfect love will dispel your fears. I do not bring trials without an escape. I do not bring a torrential rain with no promise of a rainbow. I do not leave you alone in your despair. I go with you, holding your hand, as we walk together through the storm.

Do not be downcast longer than necessary. I will follow your times of sorrow with times of greater joy. You belong to me. I will not let you suffer unnecessarily. Open your eyes, and embrace a new day. Arise, and seek the one who made you. Relief is in your near future. Trust me, I will not forget you. Earnestly chase after me. Sweet fellowship with me will become your respite. When you are with me, my peace fills the air around you and permeates your soul. Your sorrow will soon melt away. Your grief will fade with the daylight.

I am your God. I am your safe place. Come to me, and let me love you. Rest in me, and I will take care of you. Stay close to me; my protection is your fortress. Look to me first; I will be your guide. Regard me always. I will lead you in my chosen path for you. Do not hold on to worry. Cast all your troubles on me. I will carry your load.

Look unto the heavens. I am there. Before you and behind you, my protection hems you in. My compassions do not fail you. You are the one I delight in. Take refuge in me. Your future with me is secure. I have cleared the road ahead of you. Be confident in my ways. Trust in me with all your heart. Acknowledge me, and I will make your paths straight.

"Blessed is she who has believed that what the Lord has said to her will be accomplished!" (Luke 1:45)

Believe Me

Do you find it difficult to believe what I say? What causes you to doubt me? Perhaps you have been let down by people you love who have made empty promises to you. You have been led astray by people who do not have your best interests in mind. You have been abandoned by a trusted friend in your hour of need. You have been left to fend for yourself because nobody else will take care of you properly. You hold onto control because you cannot bear further disappointment in those you depend on. I understand your doubts.

I am none of those things. I am the Lord your God. I will not let you down; I keep my promises. I will not lead you astray; I lead you down paths of righteousness for my name's sake. I will never leave you or forsake you in your hour of need. I am with you always. You do not have to be so strong; I will protect you and take care of you. Let go. I am in control. You can count on me. I will not disappoint you. I am the one who created you to love you. You are my beloved child. You can depend on me for all your needs. I will provide for you.

You are blessed when you believe what I tell you will be accomplished. I do not ask you to have faith in weak people who will most definitely disappoint you. I ask you to trust in me, believe me, and my will shall be done. I will do as I say, whether you believe me or not; but when you believe me, you will experience abundant blessings. My words are not empty. They do not come back to me void. I speak, and the world obeys my commands. I spoke the world into existence.

Try putting your trust in me completely. Give me a chance. Bad things happen in the world, and I allow it for the good of those who love me; but I will never leave you to fend for yourself. I wait for you to run to me, and depend on me for your life. It is during these difficult times that you understand how much you mean to me. You appreciate my promises to be true. You see that you are really not in control; but I am in command of all things.

The next time you hear my voice will you be ready to listen? Will you believe that what I say to you will be accomplished? Blessed be the one who believes wholeheartedly. Be expectant with the confidence of knowing I am who I say I am. I am Lord of lords and King of kings; yet you call me Father. I am the Most High God—holy, holy, holy, yet you have direct access to me. I am the Savior of the world, yet you call me your friend. I AM. Believe what I say.

Morning by morning, O Lord, you hear my voice; morning by morning I lay my requests before you and wait in expectation. (Psalm 5:3)

Morning by Morning

Morning by morning I love to see your face. I love to hear your voice and listen to your requests. Please continue to lay them before me each day. You wait patiently as I prepare the way for you. It is so important that you remain faithful to me. I know what is best for you. My timing is perfect. My answers are flawless.

If you were to rush ahead of me and make your own way, you may be all right, but it may not be the *best* way for you. I am your God. I created you to love you; I will guide you in my ways. You will know my best for you when you ask and wait expectantly for my reply. Lay your requests before me, and then listen for the answer. You will hear my voice when you quiet your surroundings and your mind enough to hear my whispers.

Trust me. I am your Father in heaven. I am Lord over all creation. I am trustworthy, and I will take care of you. I will not disappoint you. I will not abandon you. I am here for you always, even to the end of the age. I will orchestrate my plans whether or not you ask me for anything, but keep asking. I love to hear your prayers. I love to hear your voice. I love it when you take time to be with me, to talk to me, and to listen to me.

Present your requests with thanksgiving. My peace will guard your heart and mind. I know what you need before you ask, but your personal growth is developed in the asking. Be patient in your waiting. I will be true to you. I have the answer for every question. Let my responses be your guide. Walk in the way I will show you. Narrow is the path I lead you on. Do not depart from it. Trouble lies on either side. Walk with me. My ways are higher than your ways. Lean on me, and I will direct you. Trust me, and I will prosper you—not with riches and fame, but with wisdom and knowledge. This is the wealth to behold.

The Lord is a refuge for the oppressed, a stronghold in times of trouble. Those who know your name will trust in you, for you, Lord, have never forsaken those who seek you. (Psalm 9:9-10)

A Stronghold in Times of Trouble

I, the Lord of all, am a refuge for the damaged and defeated soul. I am a sanctuary for the broken-hearted. I provide a place of safety for those who are crushed in spirit. They will find their respite in me. The hopeless will come to me, and I will renew a right spirit within them. Are you in the midst of trouble? Come to me for your refuge. I am in control.

Will you trust me? You can depend on me. I will not leave your side. I do not abandon those who seek me. You know my name. Put your trust in me. I will not fail you. I will not disappoint you. I am your friend in times of trouble—a good friend indeed. I will stay close to you, and give you my strength. I will see you through your times of trial. I will bring you safely through the flames—I will even carry you.

Are you hungry? I will sustain you. Are you thirsty? I will provide you with living water. Do you know me? I am your Father. You are my child. I have given you the right to call on my name. I hear your cries for help. I will not leave you alone in your times of trouble. I am by your side at all times. Do you see me? Look closely into the situation you are in. Do you see me now? I have been there all along. I will not leave you or forget about you.

Put your wholehearted trust in me. Trust me at all times, for all things. I will deliver you from evil. I will shelter you from the storm. I will walk through fire for you. I have laid down my life for you. I am your Savior. Have you put your trust in me? Do you seek me earnestly? Do you call me your Lord? Do you trust me with all your heart? You can count on me. I am your stronghold in times of trouble. You can do all things through me. I will give you strength. I will see you through your times of tribulation. Rely on me with the assurance that I am your God and King. I am your strength and shield. I AM.

"But blessed is the man who trusts in the Lord, whose confidence is in him. He will be like a tree planted by the water that sends out its roots by the stream. It does not fear when heat comes; its leaves are always green. It has no worries in a year of drought and never fails to bear fruit." (Jeremiah 17:7-8)

Put Your Confidence in the Lord

Blessed are you, my child, when you put your trust in me. Do not put your faith in the workings of man, but in the Lord alone. Put your confidence in me, and I will come through for you. I formed your body from the dust of the ground, and gave you the breath of life. Even though you sinned against me, I created an escape for your sin. My grace was sufficient for you, and you believed in me. I gave you my Spirit to bring life to your spirit.

When you trust in me, you will be like a tree I have planted near the stream of life. The roots of your foundation stretch out to reach the living water. Drink deeply from this stream of living water, and you will never thirst again. You will not fear the drought because you have been watered by me. The heat will not destroy you because my life is in your blood. You do not worry in the dry years because my living water permeates you and sustains your life.

Blessed are you, my child, when you put your trust in me. Your leaves are always green, and you never fail to bear fruit. Your appearance is rich and healthy. My life is found in you. The fruit of my Spirit is produced in its season. Your witness bears my fruit in abundance. There is no lack in your life. You want for nothing. All you have is provided by me.

Strong winds may push against your trunk, but my foundation holds you firmly to the ground. Lightning may strike at your branches, but my strength prevails in you. Pests and disease may attack your leaves, but your spiritual health and vigor remain secure with me. I will prune you to promote your growth; but your trust remains with me still. Put your confidence in me. You will be blessed to be a blessing, and bear much fruit.

I waited patiently for the Lord; he turned to me and heard my cry. He lifted me out of the slimy pit, out of the mud and mire; he set my feet on a rock and gave me a firm place to stand. He put a new song in my mouth, a hymn of praise to our God. Many will see and fear and put their trust in the Lord. Blessed is the man who makes the Lord his trust, who does not look to the proud, to those who turn aside to false gods. (Psalm 40:1-4)

A New Song

What's that? I hear you calling my name. I am here, my child. I hear your cries. You have been waiting patiently for me, but I have been here all the time. You find yourself in a difficult situation. You feel stuck and all alone, but I am here with you. You know you can depend on me. I will pull you out of the pit you are in, and set your feet on solid ground. A new song I will put on your lips, a song of praise to my name. I have rescued you from your peril again, so you lift up your praises to me.

I will use your time of difficulty, and turn it into a good thing. When others see the outcome of your struggle, they too will put their trust in me. You were at rock bottom. You called on me, and I rescued you. They will see I have turned your mourning into joy. I turned your wailing into dancing. Your woes have become rejoicing; your sorrow gave way to happiness. The transformation in your countenance is refreshing in the sight of man. Your heart sings a new song. You exalt my name and give me thanks.

Blessed is the person who trusts in the Lord. Do not imitate the ways of the self-righteous. Do not follow the one who chases after other gods; he is chasing after the wind, running toward his own destruction. Depend on me alone, and I will see you through your times of trouble. I have brighter days ahead for you. You will tell of my faithfulness and my salvation. You will tell of the wonders I have done. Do not seal your lips; let your voice be heard by all. Recount my goodness and mercy to the gathering. When you put your trust in me, others will do the same. Sing a new song of praise to the Lord your God.

May the God of hope fill you with all joy and peace as you trust in him, so that you may overflow with hope by the power of the Holy Spirit. (Romans 15:13)

Overflow with Hope

My beloved one, I know how difficult it is at times to put your trust in me. I designed you with self-confidence so that you could carry out my will, but being confident in your own identity does not mean you cannot rely on me. Your identity is found in me. You are my creation. You are made in my image. I gave you dominance over the earth, but I also created an order to the universe. Every living thing reports to someone. The husband is the head of the wife; Christ is the head of the man; and Christ willingly submits himself to me. I am in control of all things.

Submit yourself to me, and I will fill you with joy and peace as you trust in me. You will experience great joy when you are obedient to me. Your spirit will find contentment when you submit yourself to my Spirit. Delight yourself in me, and I will fill your heart with my goodness. The God of peace will create a peaceful spirit within you. You will have the calm assurance of knowing that I am in control, and I want the best for you. I will quiet the storms around you when you put your trust in me. I am your anchor of hope.

By my Spirit, your hope will overflow when you put your faith in me. I am worthy of your trust. Anticipate an eternity with me because you have the hope of eternal life. Expect my goodness to permeate your life when you depend on me. It is not a sign of weakness to rely on the God of hope. In your weakness, you will be made strong. I am the strength you put your confidence in. I will renew your strength. My peace is within your grasp when you entrust yourself to me. May your spirit overflow with the joy, peace, and hope that come from committing yourself to me.

"I have told you these things, so that in me you may have peace. In this world you will have trouble. But take heart! I have overcome the world." (John 16:33)

Take Heart!

In the middle of your chaos, focus your mind and attention on me. I am at the center of your being. In me you will find peace amidst the toil and trouble of the day. I am with you now and always. All you need to do is ask. Ask for my wisdom. Ask for my comfort. Ask for my presence. Ask for my protection. Ask for my guidance. Ask for my joy. Whatever you desire, ask for it in my name, and my Father will give it to you.

Walls may crumble down around you. The earth may shake and the thunder roll, but I am your anchor in the storm. Cling to me; I am your stronghold in times of trouble. Your sadness is not without cause, but I will exchange your grief for joy. When the storm is over, you will rejoice again in my name. I give you all you stand in need of. My provision is greater than your need.

When you are weak, it is my strength that pulls you through. When you are lost, you will be found by me. When you are depressed, I will remove your sackcloth, and clothe you with joy. Do not be afraid, for I am with you. Never give up! I am your partner in affliction. I am your companion in grief. There will be trouble in this world, but behold, I have overcome the world. Nothing could keep me in the grave. I am alive, and I live in you.

You may experience my peace at all times. Whether you are in a battle or resting in a bunker, my peace is yours to hang on to. You may rest in the knowledge that I am in control of all things. I have your best interests in mind, and I will see you through your present difficulty. Take heart! Your God is with you. The peace of God which passes understanding will carry you through your times of tribulation. Together, we will be triumphant.

"Do not let your hearts be troubled. Trust in God; trust also in me. In my Father's house are many rooms; if it were not so, I would have told you. I am going there to prepare a place for you. And if I go and prepare a place for you, I will come back and take you to be with me that you also may be where I am. You know the way to the place where I am going." (John 14:1-4)

Trust in God

Do not be concerned about your life after this world. You have entrusted yourself to me. You are using your life to fulfill my purpose in God's kingdom here on earth, but on the day and hour God determines, the life you know now, will come to an end. Do not be anxious; a greater life awaits you. I have gone ahead of you to prepare a place for you in heaven. I will return to you someday, and bring you to the place I have prepared for you. I want you to spend eternity with me and my Father.

Put your trust in my Father and in me. My Father's house accommodates many people, but there is only one way to reach my Father's house. I am the way. If you know me, you know the way to my Father. I am in my Father, and my Father is in me. Follow me, and I will lead you to the throne of God, both in this life and in the next. My Father sent me to do his work. I have accomplished what I was sent to do and returned to my Father's side.

Do not fret about tomorrow. Your tomorrow rests in my hands. Worrying will not add a moment to your life. Cast all your burdens in my direction. Seek my Father before anything else, above all else. He provides everything you ever need or want. My Father's will is set on all good things. Nothing is impossible. Approach God's throne of grace with thanksgiving on your lips. He has fed you, clothed you, and provided you with shelter; but even more than that, he has given you abundant life, even life eternally in his presence.

Do not be set in your own ways, but look first to my Father in heaven. He knows all things and has determined what is best for you. He marks the way of the righteous and leads them down his chosen path for his name's sake. Follow his lead. Trust in God completely.

But he said to me, "My grace is sufficient for you, for my power is made perfect in weakness." Therefore I will boast all the more gladly about my weaknesses, so that Christ's power may rest on me. That is why, for Christ's sake, I delight in weaknesses, in insults, in hardships, in persecutions, in difficulties. For when I am weak, then I am strong. (2 Corinthians 12:9-10)

My Grace is Sufficient for You

My precious child, my favor remains upon you. I bless you with my mercy and loving kindness. My grace is adequate for each difficulty you face. My influence is most dominant when I use an empty, broken vessel. When you are drained, I fill you with my Spirit. I seal you by the power of my Spirit for my good work. My strength pours out of the cracks in your exterior. My power is made great in the midst of your weakness.

If you were flawless, you would have no need of me. No demonstration of my power is revealed through the self-sufficient one. Be not proud in your independence, but boast with enthusiasm about your weaknesses, and my power will rest on you. Delight in the hardships you face. Your adversity is the window to my authority. The difficulties that challenge you are the perfect opportunities for me to prove my might. I will work with your imperfections because my power is completed in you.

My grace is sufficient for you. When you trust me for your strength, I will not leave you in your weakness. I am enough for you. Do not be ashamed to depend on me. When you lean on me, I am your rock. When you call to me, I hear your cry. When your trial is too much for you to bear, I am with you. The thorn in your side may torment you, but my power is made perfect in weakness. My grace is enough for you to remain strong. The trials you walk through bring you closer to me. Have faith in me, and I will carry you through. Rely on me alone for your strength. My might shows through your helplessness. My grace is sufficient for you. Trust in my omnipotence. I am unstoppable.

And we have seen and testify that the Father has sent his Son to be the Savior of the world. If anyone acknowledges that Jesus is the Son of God, God lives in him and he in God. And so we know and rely on the love God has for us. God is love. (1 John 4:14-16a)

Rely on My Love

You are my adopted sons and daughters. You live in me, and I live in you. You can rely on my love. I have proven it for you. I loved you enough to send my only Son to bear the burden of your sin, and save you from the punishment you deserved. My love will not let you down. You can count on my love to get you through the most difficult circumstances. Can you grasp the measure of my love for you?

My love surpasses your comprehension. It is wider than the expanse of the heavens. My love for you is extensive in length, stretching outside the boundaries of this world. It soars to new heights that you cannot see or imagine. The depth of my love reaches far beyond the ocean's bottom and the earth's core. Do you understand how much I love you?

My love for you is demonstrated through my Son. Rely on my Son, and rely on my love. The Spirit who lives inside you will teach you about my love and remind you of my loving kindness. You are being transformed daily by my Spirit and my love. Trust in the greater things. My love is greater than anything you will ever know.

Since I have loved you so much, you should love one another. Man has not seen me with his own eyes, but if you love each other, I am alive in you. My love is made complete when you love another. When you live in me, I live in you. My perfect love drives out your fears. Your punishment has been removed by me. If, however, you do not love your brother, you do not love me. If you do not love one you can see, how can you love the one you cannot see? If you love me, you must also love your brothers and sisters. I am love. Rely on me in order to love like I love. You can do all things through me. Rely on my love.

"'If you can'?" said Jesus. "Everything is possible for him who believes." Immediately the boy's father exclaimed, "I do believe; help me overcome my unbelief!" (Mark 9:23-24)

Overcome Your Unbelief

My beloved one, I understand your lack of trust. Trust is a virtue of great value. You have been let down so many times by the ones you love. I do not ask you to put your trust in someone that will most certainly disappoint you. I ask you to put your trust in me, the God of the universe. Have confidence that I will keep my promises to you. I will not fail you. I will not abandon you. I will not disappoint you. I am trustworthy.

I am the truth. You may believe everything that comes from my mouth. I know you want to believe me and trust me in your heart. It is your head that stands in your way. You hold on to the disappointment you have known. You cling to the idea that you may rely on no one else. You have had to look after yourself all your life. Stop! I am here. I have been here all the time. You can put your hope and trust in me. I will keep you safe; I will protect you.

Look into each of the memories you hold on to. Do you see me? Look more closely. I am there. I have been with you the entire time. You did not see me, because you did not believe in me. Now that you know me, do you see me? I have walked with you through the fire. I have sheltered you from the storms. I do not let destruction take you over. I have protected you from your enemies.

Consider what I have done for you. I willingly laid down my life for you. If you were the only person on the earth, I still would have died for your sake. Does just anyone do that? No. I am the Lord your God, and you are mine. When you take the time to know me better, you will see me, and your faith will increase. Until then, accept what I say is true. Everything is possible when you believe. I know you want to believe. I will help you overcome your unbelief.

Do not be anxious about anything, but in everything, by prayer and petition, with thanksgiving, present your requests to God. And the peace of God, which transcends all understanding, will guard your hearts and your minds in Christ Jesus. (Philippians 4:6-7)

Do Not Be Anxious

My loving child, I have given you what you first asked me for. Your life has been changed by me, and now you kneel before me again. Your prayers do not go unheard; I listen to each one, but the answer will not come in the timeframe you desire. It is all in my perfect timing. You have done your part. You have submitted yourself to me. You have asked for my help. You are faithful in your prayers. Now, you need to leave this one to me.

Return to your place of worship, and live the life I have called you to. Be sure that your own house is kept tidy, before you try to clean the home of another. Do you try to remove the speck from your brother's eye when there is a plank in your own? You do what you need to do to stay close to me, and leave this one to me. I will do what I must when the time is right. Be patient in endurance. Remember, I am in control.

Place this one at my feet and walk away. This belongs to me. Do not give in to the desires of the flesh, but put your hope in me. Nothing is impossible with me. My transforming power will be seen in due time. Keep up with the tasks I have given you. Believe in me. Follow me. Listen to me. Trust me. Feast on me. Remain in my Word. Obey my commands. Experience me. Live in my Spirit. Remain in me. Proclaim me. Glorify me. Love me first. Love others as I have loved you. Do these things, and your life will be long.

When you diligently work at pleasing me, you will be too busy to worry. Place your concerns in my capable hands, and leave the rest to me. Do not be anxious about anything. With thanksgiving, make your requests known to me. I will carry the burden of your appeals before the God of all creation. Assemble your patience for the process; put your trust in me.

Those who trust in the Lord are like Mount Zion, which cannot be shaken but endures forever. (Psalm 125:1)

Like a Mountain

My blessed one, when you trust in me, you are like a mountain that cannot be shaken. You are like Mount Zion, which lasts forever. Put your trust in me, and you will not be traumatized by anything that comes your way. The element of surprise will not frighten you when you depend on the Lord. Earthquakes will come and go, but your foundation will remain strong and intact. Waves may crash against you, but your surface will not be eroded by them.

Does it feel awkward to trust in me completely? Do you find it difficult to relinquish your control to me? Think about this. Do you give over your power to me or do I give over my power to you? I rule over all things whether you believe it or not. Get rid of the deception that causes you to feel that you have dominance in any situation, except that which I give you. Your dominion over the birds of the air and the fish of the sea was given to you by me. Humble yourself in the sight of the Lord, for the Lord despises the self-righteous person, but gives grace to the lowly, unassuming one.

Like a mighty mountain, you will not crumble and fall into the sea at the first sign of disaster. You will remain forever in my strength. Your constitution will not waiver. Your foundation in me is sure. Stay true to me. My love for you endures all things. My power is immeasurable. I protect you and keep you from evil. I provide you with everything you need. I have your well-being in mind. I know the future. You are safe with me. I am steadfast. My love is unconditional. I will never fail you. You can depend on me. I am like a mighty mountain. I will not be shaken. I will not fall. I will outlast everything on this earth.

Command those who are rich in this present world not to be arrogant nor to put their hope in wealth, which is so uncertain, but to put their hope in God, who richly provides us with everything for our enjoyment. (1 Timothy 6:17)

Put Your Hope in God

My beloved one, learn to be content with what you have in this world. Do not seek the riches of this life, but lay up for yourself the treasure of a firm foundation in Christ for the life that is to come. Financial wealth on this earth is so unsure. When you love money, and all that it buys, more than you love me, surely evil is the basis of your misconception. You have been robbed of the truth. Money will not bring you the happiness you desire. Do not be overconfident and put your hope in earthly comforts. You came into the world empty handed, and you will take nothing with you into the next life.

You may be rich by the measures of today, but will you be rich in the world to come? Though you possess the wealth of men, you may be poor in the things of God. Practice doing good, and be generous with what you own. Share your present wealth with those who are needy, and accumulate your wealth in the life to come. Then you may embrace the life that is truly life.

Food and clothing are all that you need to be content. Do not fall into the trap of desiring greater wealth. It could be the cause of your eternal destruction. If money brings you much excitement, it could also rob you of your joy. Material possessions do not secure your future in heaven. Do not delight in your money, but delight yourself in the Lord. Be pleasing to God, and he will bless you with the desires of your heart. Put your hope in God who so luxuriously supplies you with everything you need for your great pleasure.

A furious squall came up, and the waves broke over the boat, so that it was nearly swamped. Jesus was in the stern, sleeping on a cushion. The disciples woke him and said to him, "Teacher, don't you care if we drown?" He got up, rebuked the wind and said to the waves, "Quiet! Be still!" Then the wind died down and it was completely calm. (Mark 4:37-39)

I Will Quiet the Storm

My precious one, I am with you in the midst of the tempest. I am with you at all times. I will never leave you. You can call on me any time, day or night. I am always at your side. Storms will form in your life. Some will be fierce. Do not be afraid, for I am here. I will rebuke the wind that tosses your vessel. I will quiet the waves that crash against you. I am the Lord of all. Even the wind and the waves obey me. I will calm your storm and reassure you in your fears. Your comfort is found in me alone. We will ride out this storm together.

Do you trust me? Do you believe that I am in control? Will you remember to call on me first before you sail into the squalls ahead of you? Sometimes I wait for you to come to me. I do not always interfere in your life. I patiently linger until I hear from you. I want you to know that you can depend on me. I will protect you from harm. I will not always rescue you or remove your troubles from you, but I will remain with you, and lead you through the difficult times.

Some trials teach great lessons that mature you in your faith. I would not want to steal away from you an important learning opportunity. I will not allow you to experience more suffering than you can endure. I will strengthen you to do all things. I am the rock you may rest upon. I am your fortress in the battle. I will calm the wind and the waves before your vessel is compromised. My child, I am with you. I bear your burden. I suffer with you. I cry when you cry. I will quiet you with my love. You are my child, most precious. I am always here for you. Seek me in the storm. I will bring you peace in the middle of your struggle. I will quiet the storm inside you.

The angel answered, ". . . For nothing is impossible with God." "I am the Lord's servant," Mary answered. "May it be to me as you have said." Then the angel left her. (Luke 1:37-38)

Nothing is Impossible

My chosen one, you are highly favored by me. I have chosen you to carry out my will because you have a servant's heart. You will do that which seems impossible because I will provide the way. Nothing is impossible with me. I am the God of the universe. I created the heavens and the earth and everything in them. I know all things. All power belongs to me. I am everywhere at all times. I am the King of kings and Lord of lords, Almighty God; and yet I call you my child. You belong to me. You are the heir to my throne.

In spite of all this power, I humbled myself and took on human form, so that I could offer you a path of reconciliation. Your sin separated us, but I provided the sacrificial Lamb to be the atonement for your sins. I paid the price of your redemption. You have accepted me as your Savior and your Redeemer. I exchanged my life for yours. You will not suffer the punishment your sins deserved.

Humble yourself for the task I give you, and I will raise you up. Revere me, and I will do great things for you. Wait on me for your instructions. I will lead you down the path of righteousness. Blessed are you in your meekness. I will extend my mercy to all generations that come after you because you respect my power, and honor me with your service. I give strength to the weak and wisdom to the unassuming. Serve me with a heart that is glad. Do not grumble as you do my work. Do not complain about the task you have been given.

Trust in me with all of your heart. Love me the same way. You will do all things in the strength I give you. My power is not for the faint of heart. Be strong in the Lord and ready to take on my challenges. Put your hope in me, and you will soar on wings like eagles. You will run and not grow weary; you will walk and not be faint. Nothing is impossible for you when you are in me.

Chapter 5

FEAST ON ME

He is all we need. When we feast on his words,
we will never hunger or thirst again.

"So he got up and went to his father. But while he was still a long way off, his father saw him and was filled with compassion for him; he ran to his son, threw his arms around him and kissed him." (Luke 15:20)

Feast on Me

My child, I have been waiting for this day for so long now. I see you off in the distance. I know your heart. Come home, my child. You are always welcome at my table. Do you see me? I am running out to greet you. My arms are open wide. I love you. I can't wait to hold you in my arms. Welcome home, child. Welcome home. This deserves a celebration.

I have prepared a feast for you—a feast that you have never seen before. You are weary from your travels. Come, my child, rest in me. Your clothes are like filthy rags. My robe of righteousness awaits you. Your feet are dusty from the path you were on. Let me wash you whiter than snow. Here are my ring and my sandals, child. Wear them as if they were your own. You are my child, and you have returned to me. Let's celebrate! You were far off, and now you are home.

I have been there with you all along, my child. I have been with you every step of your journey. I know every word you will speak to me, but I cannot wait to hear it from you. You must tell me everything. I have all the time in the world for you. Come, sit with me; let's talk. I can't wait to hear your voice again. I have missed you, my child. I have missed our daily talks.

But first, let's take care of your needs. You are weary from your journey, and your belly groans with hunger for food that is satisfying. I have prepared a feast for you, my child, and the feast is ready. I am the feast. I am all you need. Only I will satisfy your hunger. Only I will satisfy your thirst. Sit with me; eat and drink until you are full. Eat, drink, and be satisfied with me.

"The fear of the Lord is the beginning of wisdom, and knowledge of the Holy One is understanding." (Proverbs 9:10)

Know Me

Do not fear me as you would fear being alone in a cage with a hungry lion, but fear me out of reverence for me. You fear the lion because you know he is dangerously powerful. He is strong, confident, and his jaws are crushing. His fierce brawn, along with the mane he boasts around his head, entitles him to be called, "king of the jungle."

I am the lion of Judah—the King of kings. I am strong, confident, and powerful, too. What distinguishes me from the lion you fear is that I love you, and desire the best for you. I would not hurt you or devour you. You are my beloved child—my own creation.

I desire your reverence. Respect my strength and my power. I can move mountains and cause them to crumble into the sea, but I care for you deeply, and would not use my power maliciously to destroy you. Your admiration of me is the establishment of your wisdom. When you know me, you will understand me. When you know me and understand me, my wisdom is available to you. Ask me for my wisdom, and I will give it to you freely. Respect me, and my knowledge will be granted to you.

To know me and understand me, spend time with me each day. The more time you spend with me, the better you know me. The better you know me, the better you will understand me. I am with you always. I know you better than you know yourself, but I still desire to spend as much time as possible with you each day, because I love you. You bring me great joy when you seek me and talk to me. When you delight yourself in me, I will give you the desires of your heart. I love to hear your voice—do you love to hear mine? I love to just "be" with you. Give your time and your heart to me, and you will be wise. My wisdom is available to all who know me.

To the man who pleases him, God gives wisdom, knowledge and happiness, but to the sinner he gives the task of gathering and storing up wealth to hand it over to the one who pleases God. This too is meaningless, a chasing after the wind. (Ecclesiastes 2:26)

Wisdom, Knowledge, and Happiness

My child, is it happiness you desire? Delight in me, listen to my words, and obey my commands. My lasting joy will fill your heart. I do not withhold good gifts from those who seek to satisfy me. Is it wisdom and knowledge you wish to have? Gratify me, and my wisdom will grace your head. Please me, and wear my knowledge like a wreath around your neck.

For your reverence, you will be rewarded with my wisdom. Knowledge is a gift from above. Happiness of heart is a result of your obedience to my requests. Do you understand what I say? Have you heard my voice and obeyed my instructions? Listen to me. Carry out my urges. Complete my directions. No greater satisfaction you will find than the remuneration you receive for your submission to me.

Nothing pleases me more than your adoration, devotion, and trust. I am worthy of your praise. I vie for your time and affection. Approach me with your faith and hope. Expect the greatness that you search for. I will not fail you. I am everything you need. You will share in the abundance of your inheritance. You are my child. I will take care of you.

Happiness, wisdom, and knowledge will adorn your heart and mind. Make your requests known to me, and I will shower you with the excellent gifts I have to give you. Remain upright and live a virtuous life, your reward awaits you in eternity. Carry out my commands, and receive the honor of a life well lived.

But if you decide to remain in your sin, your toil will be in vain. You will not receive the rewards of your work. You will be working for the one who pleases me. Your labor will store up wealth to be turned over to the one who gratifies me. It is a meaningless life chasing after the wind. Turn away from your sin, and choose a plentiful life of happiness in me. Feast on me and my words, you will never be hungry or thirsty again.

"The thief comes only to steal and kill and destroy; I have come that they may have life, and have it to the full." (John 10:10)

Abundant Life

Stay alert, my beloved one. Your battle is not with flesh and blood, but with the evil forces in this dark world. My enemy wants to see your demise—death of your body, but even more, he wants to see the death of your soul. He comes to steal you away from me. He comes to lead you astray. The thief comes to destroy your heart and your commitment to me. I have come so that you may have life—a full life in this kingdom and the next. When you believe in me, not only will you have a rich, meaningful life on this earth, you will also experience eternal life with me.

What is a full life? A peaceful life is worth more than words can describe. Peace comes from knowing me and trusting me. I am in control. I will take care of you. I have your best interests in mind. Believe me. I have a plan for you. I am always with you. A plentiful life is a life where all your needs are met. You have ample food, water, shelter, clothing, and more. You have exactly what you need to survive and then some. A Spirit-filled life is living a life in tune with the Holy Spirit that lives inside you. He speaks to you, protects you, guides you, convicts you, restores you, teaches you, comforts you, and loves you. There is no better friend than the Spirit of God. An abundant life produces good fruit. Fruit is the visible result of living a Spirit-filled life in Christ.

Are you happy? Are you content in any situation you are in—whether well-fed or hungry, rich or poor, alone or surrounded by friends? Are you thankful for the little things in life? You came into the world with nothing, and you will leave it with nothing. You have all you need in me. I am the good shepherd who laid down his life for his friends. My generous grace is sufficient for you. A full life is a life full of me. Feast on me. Are you full yet?

"He who has an ear, let him hear what the Spirit says to the churches. To him who overcomes, I will give some of the hidden manna. I will also give him a white stone with a new name written on it, known only to him who receives it." *(Revelation 2:17)*

Hidden Manna

Listen to me, my child. Lend your ear to my sayings. Hear the voice of my Spirit calling out to you. Remain true to me. Do not give in to the world's desires. Do not partake in the devices of evil. Live a virtuous life committed to my name. Do not renounce me when the world rushes in on you. Stand firm in the days of disaster. Do not listen to the false prophets and teachers who claim to know me. They speak words of evil disguised with the sweet nectar of honey.

In those days, you will return to me. Approach my throne in humility. Open my Word, and search for your protection. My suit of armor awaits you. Grab hold of the shield of faith, and guard your heart. Give no evil an open door to your soul. Sharpen your sword, and know the Word of God. Proudly wear the breastplate of righteousness. It is for my name's sake. Ready your feet with the gospel of peace—proclaim my salvation wherever your feet take you. Stand firm in the truth; wear it as a belt around your waist. Clothe yourself in my salvation, as a helmet that protects your head. Let wisdom and discernment be your guide. Wrap everything in prayer, allowing the Spirit to lead you as you pray.

Remain faithful to my name. Repent and overcome the desires of the flesh. Then you will enjoy some of the manna which is hidden from those who do not uphold my name. The secret manna will satisfy your hunger. Your temptation will not conquer you. Sweet victory will grace you as a garland. I will call you by a new name. Only you will recognize it. Strength and honor will carry you through the days of challenge. Feast on my words. Enjoy the satisfaction of knowing me.

And this is his command: to believe in the name of his Son, Jesus Christ, and to love one another as he commanded us. Those who obey his commands live in him, and he in them. And this is how we know that he lives in us: We know it by the Spirit he gave us. (1 John 3:23-24)

I Live in You

Nothing will bring you more comfort and confidence than knowing that I live in you. From the moment you proclaimed that you believe in my Son, I sent my Holy Spirit to live in your heart. Never again shall you hunger or thirst. You have a living feast within your soul. Are you hungry for God? My Spirit will satisfy your cravings. Do you thirst after me? My Spirit will quench your dryness. You need only to call on my name. I will answer anytime, day or night. You have the living God, living in you.

When you live in me by obeying my commands, I will live in you. When I live in you, I ask you to abide by me. You must not only believe in my Son, Jesus Christ, you must also love one another. I loved you first, now you must love another with my love. If you do not love, you do not know me. I am love. If you love each other, I live in you, and my love is made complete in you. Others will see my love when they see you loving another as I have loved you. They will see that I am in you, and you are in me.

Do you have someone in your life that is difficult to love? I tell you, love him or her anyway. Love him as I love him. Love her as I love you. Has it always been easy for me to love you? I love you no matter what. My love is unconditional. I do not love you based on who you are or what you have done. I love you because I created you. I love you because you are made in my image. I love you because I am love. So you ought to love the unlovable. Love that person who is impossible to love. Search me and know that I loved him first. Give love a chance. You will be amazed at the transforming power that love has. You have been transformed by my love. You have the ability to love unconditionally because I live in you.

And this is the testimony: God has given us eternal life, and this life is in his Son. He who has the Son has life; he who does not have the Son of God does not have life. (1 John 5:11-12)

Life in the Son

You say you love me; then, you love my Son as well. I have given my Son for you that you may have life. When I sent my Son to die for you, I provided the way to eternal life. Jesus Christ is that way. He is the only way to life in me. When you have the Son, you have life—not just life, but life eternal. If you do not have the Son, you have no life. Have you accepted my Son as your Savior? Do you have the life I offer you?

When Christ died for you, he asked me to send my Spirit to live in you. This way, your life would not be empty and void. When you have the Spirit inside you, you have life. There is life in the Spirit of God. He is your lifeblood. Everything the Spirit does and says is filtered through me and directed by me. Your life is not your own. You belong to me as the Spirit does. I will attest to this fact. Life without my Spirit is no life at all, but living in the Spirit is having the abundant life I give you. The fruit of the Spirit demonstrates to others that you belong to me, and my Spirit lives in you.

When you believe in the name of the Son of God, you know that you have eternal life. You also have the assurance of knowing that, when you approach me, if you ask for anything according to my will, you will have what you asked of me. My Son has given you the understanding of knowing the truth. I am the true God and eternal life. There is no falsehood in me. Knowing me and believing in my Son gives you the certainty of eternal life. Do not condemn yourself in your heart. You may rest in the truth of knowing me. When you belong to me, you know the truth, and the truth brings you true life. There is no better life than a true life in me. I am the truth, and the truth lives in you.

"The Lord your God is with you, he is mighty to save. He will take great delight in you, he will quiet you with his love, he will rejoice over you with singing." (Zephaniah 3:17)

I Take Great Delight in You

O daughter of the king, you will rejoice and be glad. I have removed your punishment. You shall not be afraid of anything. I have turned back your enemy. I am with you, and will never leave you. I am powerful, and I will save you. You are my child, and I delight in you greatly. You are my daughter, my precious one. I will rescue you and bring you home. I will set you free from captivity.

O child of mine, you are at home with me. I enjoy the time I spend with you. You bring me great pleasure and satisfaction. Do not let your heart be troubled. I will quiet you with my love. Do not set yourself to worry. I will remove all your cares. I will speak over you with my tender, soothing words. Listen to my gentle whispers. My voice will calm your uncertainties. I am here to protect you and save you. You have nothing to fear, for I am with you. I will not leave you alone.

O daughter of mine, you are very special to me. I will return the smile to your face. I rejoice over you with singing. My words fall quickly to your ears as you listen with great anticipation. I celebrate your presence. Your existence completes my joy. Rejoice and be glad with me. Your heart will soar to new heights. I will set you on wings of eagles. Put your hope and trust in me. I will renew your strength. I have led you out of your captivity and set you free. I will guide you, and arm you with my strength. I will surround you with my love, and protect you from your enemy.

O precious child of mine, do you know how greatly I delight in you? Let me quiet you with my love. Listen to me as I rejoice over you in song. Let the sound of my voice be your comfort. Let my whispers calm your fears and reassure you of my great love for you.

"'For this is what the Sovereign Lord says: I myself will search for my sheep and look after them. As a shepherd looks after his scattered flock when he is with them, so will I look after my sheep.'" (Ezekiel 34:11-12a)

I Look After My Sheep

I am the good shepherd. I, myself, will look after my sheep. When one sheep is lost, I will leave the other ninety-nine sheep in the open field in search of my one lost sheep; and when I find him, I will return him safely home. I will tend my flock like a good shepherd. I will gather the lambs in my arms. I will carry them around in my arms all day if I need to. I will hold them close to my heart. Though my flock may be scattered, I know where each sheep is at all times. I am with them always. I will not abandon them. I look after my sheep.

My sheep will want for nothing. Everything I have belongs to them. They will lie down in pastures of green and drink from cool, quiet waters. They will hunger and thirst no more. I will guide them and walk with them through the valleys, even the desert. They have nothing to fear; I will walk ahead of them. I will comfort them. I will protect them. I will provide for them. I will enter the sheep pen by the gate, and my sheep will follow me because they know me, and I know them. I call each one by name. They listen to my voice and follow me.

I care for my sheep as my Father cares for me. I love my sheep, and my sheep love me. When my sheep have gone astray, I lay down my life for my sheep. I lay it down of my own accord. I do it willingly because I am the good shepherd. I go to great lengths to rescue the lost. I will find the lost sheep, rescue him from the hands of his enemies, and carry him home. I wipe away all his iniquities and return him to my Father. I am the gate, the only way back to the Father. My sheep will enter the gate and find their safety in the arms of the Father. You are my sheep, and I am your shepherd. I will gather you up and carry you close to my heart.

"I tell you the truth, he who believes has everlasting life. I am the bread of life. Your forefathers ate the manna in the desert, yet they died. But here is the bread that comes down from heaven, which a man may eat and not die." (John 6:47-50)

Living Bread

My child, you work and purchase food that will eventually spoil if not eaten in a timely fashion. Do not work for such food when you can have the food that sustains your life—even life eternal. Come to me. I am the bread from heaven. I have come to give life to the world. Take and eat my bread, and you will not be hungry for the bread the world provides. My bread will sustain your life and endure to life eternal. Take, eat, and be satisfied. Taste and see that the bread from heaven is good.

Do not work for bread that eventually molds. Your hunger will not be satisfied with that bread. Eat of my bread, and you will live forever. I have given my bread, my flesh, for the life of the world. Feast on me, and you will not be hungry. Feed on me, and you will live forever because of me.

Do not search for water from a well. Believe in me, and you will never be thirsty again. Well water will not quench your thirst like my living water does. I have given my drink, my blood for the life of the world. My blood was poured out on the cross to purchase your redemption. Partake of my blood, drink from my cup, and live forever without being thirsty.

Nothing will satisfy you like the bread and the drink I provide you. Your forefathers ate manna in the desert and died. Feed on me, the living bread, and you will live forever. Believe in me, and you will have everlasting life. My life is in my flesh and blood. Eat of my flesh and drink of my blood, and you will find life in me. Eat and drink what I offer you. Remain in me, and I will remain in you. Feast on me, and you will not be hungry. Believe in me, and you will not be thirsty. I am the bread of life. Taste and see that the Lord is good, and live forever with me.

How priceless is your unfailing love! Both high and low among men find refuge in the shadow of your wings. They feast on the abundance of your house; you give them drink from your river of delights. For with you is the fountain of life; in your light we see light. (Psalm 36:7-9)

Feast on My Abundance

My dear one, I love you unconditionally. My love does not fail you. No value can be put on my love. It is priceless. My love is worth more than precious gems—more than silver or gold. My love is yours without cost to you. My great love for you was demonstrated when I gave my Son's life for you. I have loved you since before I created the world. You were in my mind; I conceived you in my thoughts. I loved you before the world began, and I will love you far beyond its end. You are mine. I have called you by name. Find your life in me.

Find your refuge in me. I am your fortress of protection. I will place you in the shadow of my wings. You have nothing to fear because I am your stronghold. I clothe you in my armor; no force can penetrate it. I surround you with my shield. I am your defender. I guard your paths and guide your steps. You may find your security in me. Your safety is my chief concern.

Come into my house and partake of the feast I have prepared for you. Eat from the abundance of my provision. Drink from the living water I give you. Find delight in the food and drink I offer you. My food and drink will sustain your life. Your hunger and thirst will be satisfied. In my house you will find the fountain of life. My fountain springs forth to life eternal. Put your faith and trust in me, and drink of the fountain of life. Believe in me—trust in my name alone—I will lead you into life everlasting.

In my light, you have seen the light. The light of my life shines for all men to see. Do not be blinded by the light, but walk in it. I am a light for your way; I will direct your paths. Come into the light, and experience life as I intended. Delight in the abundance I give you.

Acknowledge and take to heart this day that the Lord is God in heaven above and on the earth below. There is no other. (Deuteronomy 4:39)

There is No Other

Do you believe I AM? I am the only true God. There is no other God like me—never has been, never will be. I am the God in heaven, and I am the God on the earth. I am the Creator and ruler of all things. I created the heavens and the earth and every living thing. I am the one in control of everything. I spoke everything into existence, and I designed the order in the universe. I am the God of all.

I am the Lord your God. You shall have no other gods besides me. Do not worship any other god in the form of an idol or anything else. I am a jealous God; I want all of your attention. I am also a loving God. I will show love to those who love me and keep my commandments. Those who keep my commands may enjoy a long life. Be careful to obey me so that it may go well with you.

I am the Lord your God. There is no other. Love me with all your heart, soul, mind, and strength. Love me more than anything else in your life. Put me first. Make me a priority in your life. Spend time with me, and devote yourself to me. Observe my instructions. Walk in my ways. Respect me. Regard me highly. Serve me with all your heart and soul.

I am the Lord your God. There is no other. Therefore, follow my instructions. Love one another as I have loved you. Show compassion to all you know. Practice kindness, forgiveness, and understanding. Be good to my people. Do not be rude or proud. Do not be selfish, but be willing to set aside your own desires. Do not become angry easily. When you forgive, also forget. Do not keep a record of wrongs. Be truthful. Persevere in love. Do not give up on anyone. Put your trust and hope in me, and I will give you the strength to love as I do. My love does not fail. Love exceptionally. Love unconditionally. Love sacrificially. Love.

My son, do not despise the Lord's discipline and do not resent his rebuke, because the Lord disciplines those he loves, as a father the son he delights in. Blessed is the man who finds wisdom, the man who gains understanding. (Proverbs 3:11-13)

I Delight in You

My child, I delight in you. I discipline you because I love you. Do not despise my correction. Do not resent my admonishment. I must reprimand you when you go astray. I am obligated to correct you when you are disobedient. Like a good shepherd, it is my duty to hook you with my staff and bring you back in to the fold. I rescue you because I love you. I protect you from harm. Outside of the green pasture I keep you in, dangers lurk everywhere you turn. The enemy is a wolf dressed in sheep's clothing. He will entice you to wander away from me and cause you to sin.

My precious one, I delight in you. Do not ignore my teaching. Follow my instructions, and keep my commands in your heart. They will bring you longevity and prosperity. Blessed are you when you find my wisdom. A rich woman you are when you gain understanding. Wisdom and understanding are priceless treasures. Nothing you desire will compare with the wealth of knowledge. Wisdom will bring you honor and long life. The woman who chooses the path of wisdom will experience true peace.

My sweet darling, I delight in you. Trust in me with all of your heart. Acknowledge me, and I will lead you to greener pastures and cool, clear waters. I will provide you with all you need. Do not be wise in yourself, but give me your reverence. Turn away from evil, and run in my direction. I will bring health to your body and nourishment to your soul. Turn your ear to my wisdom, and accept my words. From my lips come knowledge and understanding. Walk in an upright manner. Wisdom and discernment will guard and protect you. Listen to me, and live in safety. You are the child I delight in. Delight yourself in me.

"For my flesh is real food and my blood is real drink. Whoever eats my flesh and drinks my blood remains in me, and I in him. Just as the living Father sent me and I live because of the Father, so the one who feeds on me will live because of me." (John 6:55-57)

Feed on Me

My precious child, do not be alarmed by the metaphor I have given you. I am not asking that you eat the flesh of a man and drink human blood. I am the bread from heaven. When you partake of this bread, which is my body broken for you, you commune yourself with the Holy Father. You confess that you believe I have given my body as a living sacrifice for your sin. When you partake of this drink, which is my blood, you are reconciled as one with the Holy Father. You acknowledge that my blood was spilled for your redemption from a life of sin. No longer does your sin separate you from the one true Holy God. You were bought for a price. My blood was the cost of your redemption. My body was sacrificed as payment for your sin.

When you eat of my flesh and drink of my blood, you remain in me, and I remain in you. I live forever because the Father raised me from the dead. Whoever feeds on me will live forever because of me. I invite you to feed on me. I am the feast of reconciliation. I have provided you a way back to the Father. Eat of my flesh and receive the gift of life. Drink from the cup of blessing, and claim your salvation.

I stand at your door and knock. Open the door and I will come in and dine with you, and you with me. Feed on me, and I will remain in you and give life to you. Give thanks for the feast I have provided. You will never be hungry again. Enjoy the feast my Father has prepared for you. Share the bread and the wine with those who hunger and thirst for righteousness. Proclaim the plan of salvation to those who are lost. My table is open to all who believe in me and call me Lord. Come dine with me and feast on the bread of life.

He humbled you, causing you to hunger and then feeding you with manna, which neither you nor your fathers had known, to teach you that man does not live on bread alone but on every word that comes from the mouth of the Lord. (Deuteronomy 8:3)

Man Does Not Live on Bread Alone

I have humbled you, because it is my desire that you would hunger for me. I have taken away your food and drink for a time, so that you would hunger and thirst after me. You depend on food and drink to nourish your body, but I tell you, depend on me for the nourishment for your soul. Man cannot live on bread alone, but on every word that proceeds from my mouth. My Word in Scripture and my words given to you by my Holy Spirit will fill you up until you are satisfied.

Do not become comfortable and forget what I have done for you. Do not become complacent and forget the God who delivered you. Observe my commands, and walk in my ways, as I lead you into an abundant life. You will lack nothing. You will have all the food your body needs, but what is food for the body and the body for food if a man's soul is not nourished as well. Feast on my words alone, for in them remain the secret to a life that is full. Do not rely on bread alone, but rely on me and my words to satisfy your soul.

Earnestly seek me, and plant yourself in my Word. My Spirit will water the Word you have planted in your soul, and your growth will be exponential. Remain in my Word, and my words will live in you. Just as bread sustains the body, the bread of heaven sustains the soul. Be well-fed by dining regularly in my Holy Word. Be well watered by being baptized in the Spirit. Immerse yourself in my living water, and find your refreshment in me. Eat and drink until you are satisfied—body, mind and soul.

Love is patient, love is kind. It does not envy, it does not boast, it is not proud. It is not rude, it is not self-seeking, it is not easily angered, it keeps no record of wrongs. Love does not delight in evil but rejoices with the truth. It always protects, always trusts, always hopes, always perseveres. Love never fails . . . And now these three remain: faith, hope and love. But the greatest of these is love. (1 Corinthians 13:4-8a., 13)

Love Remains

Love is the greatest gift of all. Love remains the greatest thing you have to give. I have given you my love, and loved you with everything that I am. I laid down my life for you because I love you so much. Will you lay down your life for the ones you love? Love does not seek its own ways. Deny yourself, and consider the desires of another more important than your own. Love endures all tests with its patience. Love is kind, thoughtful, and considerate, doing good only.

Love is not jealous or overconfident. Do not be envious of another, but delight in the pleasures others are given. Humble yourself, and serve one another in love. Do not be quick to anger or let your anger simmer. Do not keep track of sins or injustice, but forgive them, as your sins have been forgiven. Then let them go so that you do not become bitter. Do not take pleasure in evil, but delight in the truth.

Safeguard your love and defend it at all costs. Shield it from harm. Shelter your love from the storms. Believe in your love, and be confident in it until it proves untrustworthy. Be polite and respectful with your love. Do not treat others rudely or offensively. Anticipate the best results with your love. Aspire to greatness in all your relationships.

Do not give up on love. Love does not fail. Be persistent in your love. Keep trying to love admirably. Devote yourselves to love. Be loyal with your love. Desire the greatness of love. Do not surrender easily or admit your defeat in love. Remain true in your faith, hope, and love. Above all things, love remains. Regard love highly.

How great is the love the Father has lavished on us, that we should be called children of God! And that is what we are! The reason the world does not know us is that it did not know him. (1 John 3:1)

Children of God

You are my child. I thought of you before I created the world. I knew you before I knit you together in your mother's womb. I created you and called you blessed. I love you so much, that I traded one life for another. I gave the life of my one and only Son in exchange for your life. Jesus paid the death penalty for your sin, so that you might have a life in me. That is how much I love you, my dearest child. Do you understand the depth of my love for you? My Son laid down his life for yours. You now live and breathe in me.

I have adopted you into my kingdom. I have clothed you in righteousness. The work of Jesus on the cross has made you a priest who will serve me. My Son, the great high priest, has given you direct access to me. You are chosen, a royal priesthood, and you belong to me. You no longer need to present your gifts of sacrifice to me. Jesus is the sacrificial Lamb for all times and all peoples. Your debt has been paid.

There is no greater love for you than mine. My love for you is so wide, it spans across the land and the seas to the ends of the earth. My love for you is so long, it reaches lengths never before known to man. My love for you is so high it climbs into the heavens and returns fully back to you. My love for you is so deep, the ocean floor, thousands of feet below the surface, does not even come close to the depth of my love for you. Can you grasp it?

In love, I predestined you to be my adopted child, through Christ, in accordance with my pleasure and my will. You have been chosen by me. You have been marked with my seal, the Holy Spirit, for the day of redemption. Your royal inheritance is guaranteed. You will spend eternity with me. You will serve me in both my kingdom here on earth, and in heaven above. I have called you. You are mine. You are my precious child. You are a child of God.

This is how you can recognize the Spirit of God: Every spirit that acknowledges that Jesus Christ has come in the flesh is from God, but every spirit that does not acknowledge Jesus is not from God. This is the spirit of the antichrist, which you have heard is coming and even now is already in the world. You, dear children, are from God and have overcome them, because the one who is in you is greater than the one who is in the world. (1 John 4:2-4)

The Spirit of God

Dear child of mine, you believe in me, so I sent the Spirit of God to live in you. God, in spirit form, lives in your heart. I was conceived of the Holy Spirit and born of a woman. I grew into the full form of a man, but remained fully God also. You believe that I walked the earth in the flesh of a man. Your spirit acknowledges that fact, and now the Spirit of God lives in you.

The spirits of this dark world deny me. They do not admit that I was sent from God in the flesh. They refuse to acknowledge that I am the Son of God. Be aware of these spirits. They are not from God. Test every spirit to see if it is from my Father. Many who forecast in my name are not from me. They are from the antichrist. They do not speak the truth. They do not receive their words from God. They are crafty and deceptive.

You, my dear child, are from God. You can recognize the evil spirits. They will not take over you. You will conquer them because I live in you, and I am greater than the one who lives in the world. The world listens to the false spirits, but those who know God, will listen to you, because my Spirit of truth speaks through you. Do not grieve my Spirit, but live by my truth, and walk in my light. Get rid of any sin and wickedness. Instead, you should imitate God and his love. God delights in the man whose walk is blameless. Do not give in to the world. You live in the world, but you are a stranger to it. Do not live as the world lives because the Spirit of God lives in you.

Finally, brothers, whatever is true, whatever is noble, whatever is right, whatever is pure, whatever is lovely, whatever is admirable—if anything is excellent or praiseworthy—think about such things. Whatever you have learned or received or heard from me, or seen in me—put it into practice. And the God of peace will be with you. (Philippians 4:8-9)

Put it into Practice

My dear sister, submit your spirit to me. Be obedient to me with your thoughts and your words. In humility, acknowledge that your thoughts may not be up to my standards. You are in me. Do not live as you are in the world. Every thought you have should be detained until you have brought it before me. If you find it is not obedient to me, you must demolish it. Any thought that sets itself up against the knowledge of God should be destroyed and discarded.

My dear friend, run your thoughts through my righteous sieve. Is it true? Is it decent? Is it appropriate? Is it pure? Is it pleasant? Is it commendable? If it is excellent or worthy of praise, let it flow through your mind and into your heart. Continue to think about it. If it does not make it through my righteous sieve, it is not worthy of your time. Do not dwell on immoral ideas. Do not give the devil a stronghold by wasting one minute believing the lies he places in your head.

Instead, practice what you have seen in me and heard from me. Live out what I have taught you, the life I modeled for you. I give you many good things to ponder. Do not pay homage to the opinions of man, when you have the living God living in your heart and mind. Be respectful of my living space. Do not dirty it up with feelings of hatred, anger, rage, bitterness, jealousy, and an unforgiving spirit. Replace those feelings with love, kindness, goodness, forgiveness, compassion, mercy, patience, and peace. Decorate my dwelling place with these admirable emotions. Put into practice what I preach.

When he was at the table with them, he took bread, gave thanks, broke it and began to give it to them. Then their eyes were opened and they recognized him, and he disappeared from their sight. They asked each other, "Were not our hearts burning within us while he talked with us on the road and opened the Scriptures to us?" (Luke 24:30-32)

A Burning Heart

My precious child, you know I am with you. I am with you in Spirit at all times. I have set my Holy Spirit in your heart. The Spirit teaches you all things and reminds you about me. You are not always in tune with the Holy Spirit inside you. So, there will be times when I need to get your attention at that very moment. This is crucial. You will need to pay attention to my Spirit and obey me immediately. The Spirit takes his instruction from me and passes it along to you. Souls are at stake. Lives will be changed by the tasks I give you. It may be as simple as a witness about my goodness that you speak to the one who needs to hear it exactly then.

My dear one, when your heart burns within you, you will know. This is different than a regular bout with indigestion or acid reflux. Your heart will beat faster. Your blood pressure may increase. Your adrenaline pulses through your body telling your brain you need to act quickly. You may fear doing what you have been told to do, but I am with you. I prepare you to do what I ask of you. When you act on my instructions, you will experience my joy. Your obedience brings me great joy which spills over from my Spirit to yours. Your burning heart now burns with joy. You receive an energy-high like no other when you carry out what I ask you to do.

Just as the hearts of my disciples burned with joy when I spoke to them after my resurrection, so too, your hearts will burn within you when I speak to you, and give you an important assignment to complete. Listen to the voice of my Holy Spirit inside you. Pay attention to your physical signs that I am near. When I make a request of you, act quickly with your obedience. A heart filled with passion for me is a burning heart.

"We have here only five loaves of bread and two fish," they answered. "Bring them here to me," he said. And he directed the people to sit down on the grass. Taking the five loaves and the two fish and looking up to heaven, he gave thanks and broke the loaves. Then he gave them to the disciples, and the disciples gave them to the people. They all ate and were satisfied, and the disciples picked up twelve basketfuls of broken pieces that were left over. The number of those who ate was about five thousand men, besides women and children. (Matthew 14:17-21)

The Feast of Five Thousand

Eat and be satisfied. The bread I have broken for you will satisfy your hunger. I will give you more than you crave to meet your need. When you partake of the feast I prepare, you will not walk away empty, but yearning for more. Although you no longer hunger for food for your body, your appetite has been wetted for the food I give you, which is nourishment for your soul.

The feast I give you has been blessed by my Father. The bread which is broken for you is my body. I am the feast my Father has prepared for you. God sent me to be broken for you. The feast was designed to nurture the multitudes—men, women, and children. When all have eaten and are satisfied, the leftover pieces will feed still more people. Do not walk away from the table while you are still hungry. Stay here with me. Eat until you are satisfied.

When all your needs have been fulfilled, will you share the leftover bread with another who hungers after me? Blessed are the hungry, for they shall be satisfied. Now that you are convinced my body was broken for you, will you be able to convince another of the same? Leave that to me. You will share my feast with the poor in spirit, and I will nourish the impoverished soul. The broken bread will feed the broken-hearted. The riches of heaven will bail out the bankrupt spirit.

Are you hungry? Come to my table, for all things are ready. The feast of my Father awaits you. The bread which is broken is my body. I am the sustenance your soul requires. Feast on me. Eat until you are satisfied. Take home the leftovers to feed the poor and hungry.

Chapter 6

EXPERIENCE ME

*God describes his character
and the life modeled by his Son.*

Do you not know? Have you not heard? The Lord is the everlasting God, the Creator of the ends of the earth. He will not grow tired or weary, and his understanding no one can fathom. (Isaiah 40:28)

Creator

I am the Creator of all good things. I created the heavens and the earth, the land and the seas. I spoke plants and trees into existence. I separated day from night. I placed the sun, moon, and stars in the sky, and spoke the planets into orbit. I filled the seas with living creatures, and let the birds fly above the earth. I formed animals and livestock. I created man and woman in my own image. I am the everlasting God, the Creator of everything.

I knew you before I created you. I knit you together in your mother's womb. I created you in my own image. You were made in my likeness. You are the crown of creation. You are a reflection of me. I am the light of the world. You reflect my light to a dark and desperate world. I am the salt of the earth. Do not lose your saltiness, but remain in me. I am the living water, your lifeblood. You will never thirst again.

I am compassionate, devoted, faithful, and true. These attributes are yours to impart. I am kind and loving, merciful and patient. I empower you to ascribe to these traits. I am strong and tender. I am slow to anger and quick to forgive. Resemble me in these ways. I am the Creator of all good things. You are good, because I created you in my likeness.

By me all things were created. I do not grow tired and weary. No one can grasp my understanding. My ways are higher than your ways. Yet I call you my friend. You are my child, my heir. All that I possess is yours. I created you to love you. I love you, my child. You are blessed to be a blessing. Bless me, my love.

". . . And surely I will be with you always, to the very end of the age."
(Matthew 28:20b)

Immanuel

My beloved one, I am with you always. I am Immanuel—God with you. You have access to me 24/7. Believe that I am with you. Know that I am here. Experience all of me. Seek me and you will find me, when you seek me with all your heart. I am just a whisper away. I listen for your voice. I wait patiently to hear you call my name. I am available to you all hours of the day and night.

When you lie down to sleep, I watch over you. When you wake up in the morning, I am here. When you leave your house, I go with you. As you drive down the road, I commute with you. At the office, I sit next to your desk. When you exercise at the gym, I am there. As you fill your cart with groceries, I walk beside you. When you eat dinner with your children, I enjoy your company. I am always with you; I will never leave you. I will never forget about you.

There is no place you can hide from me. I see all you do. I know your every thought. I know the emotions you experience; I experience them with you. When you laugh; I laugh. When you cry; I cry. Your sorrow is my sorrow; your joy belongs to me. When you share your life with me, my abundant blessings are yours to behold. Ask and you will receive all I have to give you.

I love spending time with you, especially one-on-one. When we are alone, I am devoted to you only. My time is yours; my attention is as well. How can I make myself more real to you? Make time for me. Know me. Experience me in an intimate way. When you connect with me, nothing will break the bond. Nothing can penetrate our union; nothing will separate you from me. You are mine, and I am God with you—Immanuel.

"I am the good shepherd; I know my sheep and my sheep know me—just as the Father knows me and I know the Father—and I lay down my life for the sheep." (John 10:14-15)

The Good Shepherd

I am the good shepherd: I know my sheep, and my sheep know me. You are my sheep. I know you intimately. I know every breath you take, every move you make. When you go to the water to drink, I am there. When you walk along the narrow path, I am with you. When you stray from the flock, I have my eyes on you. When you get lost, I leave the flock to search for you. There is no place you can hide from me. I find you, gather you up, and carry you close to my heart. I gently lead you back home.

I am the good shepherd. I, myself, look after my sheep. I will strengthen you when you are weak. I will heal you when you are sick. I will bind up your wounds. I will rescue you when you go astray. I will bring you out of darkness into the light. I will tend you in good pasture. I will lead you to springs of living water and wipe away every tear from your eyes. You will live in safety. I will provide for you. I will equip you with everything good for doing my will.

I am the good shepherd. I call you by name. You know my voice. Listen to my voice and follow me. No one can snatch you out of my hand. I have ordained all your days. I know your thoughts. I know your heart. I give you the desires of your heart. Your heart is good like mine.

I am the good shepherd. I love my sheep, and my sheep love me. I love you so much that I took your place on the cross. I am the Lamb of God. I died for your sins. I am the shepherd that laid down his life for his sheep. I paid the ransom, and rescued you from sin and death, so that you would not perish, but live in eternity with me. I am the good shepherd.

Jesus answered, "I am the way and the truth and the life. No one comes to the Father except through me. If you really knew me, you would know my Father as well. From now on, you do know him and have seen him." (John 14:6-7)

The Way

I am the gate for the sheep. Whoever enters the gate will be saved. I am the only way to the Father. No one comes to the Father except through me. My Father has provided the way for you to come to him—through me. The curtain in the temple has been torn in two. You now have access to the Most Holy Place, the throne of God, by my own blood. You may approach God with confidence and a sincere heart because I have gone before you.

If you know me, you know my Father. If you see me, you have seen my Father. My Father and I are one. I am the Messiah, the anointed one, the Savior of the world. My Father sent me, not to condemn the world, but to save the world. When you confess that I am Lord, and you believe that God raised me from the dead, you will be saved.

God has made me a permanent priest. I will save you completely when you come to God through me because I live to intercede for you. I sit at the right hand of God, and make your requests known to him. No sin is too great to bring before God. No prayer is too small to offer him. Nothing can separate you from the love of God because I plead your case before my Father every day.

Do you understand what I have done for you, the depth of my love for you? I have made a way for you to access a holy, righteous God. I have sent my Spirit to live in your heart and guide you into all truth. You live in the center of an omnipotent triune God. You have access to power beyond your imagination. You are loved by the God of the universe. You are his child, his heir. All that he has belongs to you. I am the way. Come to me and follow me. I have prepared the way to God for you. I am the only way.

Because you are sons, God sent the Spirit of his Son into our hearts, the Spirit who calls out, "Abba, Father." So you are no longer a slave, but a son; and since you are a son, God has made you also an heir. (Galatians 4:6-7)

Abba, Father

You are my child; I am your Father. I have sent my Holy Spirit to live in your heart. My Spirit testifies with your spirit that you are my child. The Spirit calls me by my name, Abba, Father. I have made you my own daughter. I am your daddy. I love to spend time with you. I love to give you nice things. I love to provide for you. I love to protect you.

Come to me, my child. Climb up into my lap and let me cherish you. You are my beloved child; I call you my own. We have so much to talk about. We have so much to do together. Let's sit a while and catch up on your life. Let me show you my great love for you. I have made you my heir. You may have all that belongs to me. My Son has provided the way for you to come to me. Do not forsake our time together. Let me rejoice over you with singing. I will quiet you with my love. I take great pleasure being with you. You are my most precious gift. As a father delights in his children, so I am delighted in you.

Do not stray from me. I will guide you into all righteousness. I will set your feet on solid ground, and mark out the most excellent way for you. All my blessings will be yours. I will work all things together for your good. Seek me with your questions. I am the answer you search for. Your quest stops with me. I am all you need.

As a shepherd watches over his flock, I will take care of you. I will protect you from evil, and guard your life with my own. Come to me, and find your rest in me. Sit with me, and let me teach you my ways. I will let you in on my plans for you. I consider you my friend. Honor me all the days of your life. My Son brought you to me, and I have declared you my own. My Spirit lives in you and bears witness that you belong to me. I am your Father.

Then Jesus declared, "I am the bread of life. He who comes to me will never go hungry, and he who believes in me will never be thirsty." (John 6:35)

The Bread of Life

I am your *manna for today.* I am all you need. I am enough. I will satisfy your hunger. I will satisfy your thirst. I am the living bread from heaven. I give life to the world. Believe in me, feed on me, and you will live forever.

Do you desire gratification with food? How much more, then, will my bread be suitable for your soul? I am the living Word, food for your heart and mind. My flesh will satisfy your spirit. My Word will guide your feet, as a lamp unto your way. Hold on to me. Hold onto my words. My words are flawless. My words will never pass away. Remain in me, and my words will remain in you.

Does nothing quench your thirst? Follow me. I will lead you to springs of living water. Drink deeply from my well, and your soul will yearn no more. Believe in me, and streams of living water will flow from within you. My Spirit dwells within you.

I am the light of the world. In me you will find no darkness. I am the light of men, the truth for all to see. Walk in my light and bring purpose to your days. Live in the truth, and I will cleanse you from all unrighteousness. You were made in my likeness. Let your light shine for all to see. You are a reflection of me.

I am the bread of life. Come to me; you will never go hungry. Believe in me; you will never be thirsty. My life will satisfy your soul. I am the bread from heaven. I bring life to the world. I am the lifeblood that flows through your body. I bring life to your spirit. Feast on me, and you will be satisfied. Find your life in me, and live with a heart that is fully alive.

"I am the Alpha and the Omega, the First and the Last, the Beginning and the End." (Revelation 22:13)

The All-Sufficient One

Do you not know? Have you not heard? I AM. I AM the all-sufficient one. I am enough. I am the establishment and foundation of all of creation. I am the conclusion and finish of the same. I am everything in between. I am all you need.

I existed before the foundations of the earth were laid down. I was present when the moon and stars were set in the sky. I have orchestrated all of history, and I have written the script for the end of the age. I am the God who is, who was, and who is to come.

I am the Lord God Almighty. I rule and reign over every living thing. I have designed you and given you life. My darling, I am your Father in heaven and on earth. I am full of wisdom and perfect in beauty. Seek my wisdom, and I will make your ways perfect.

Come to me, my child. I have provided the way. I have seen your despair. I sent my Son to bridge the expanse between us. He pleads your case before me day and night. You may approach my throne of grace without fear and trembling. I patiently wait for you. I desire to spend time with you. I listen for your cries. I am your ever-present God.

I am King of kings and Lord of lords; Almighty is my name. I am ruler over all the earth. I am the God who loves his people. I am perfect and holy. Yet I have made you my own. You belong to me. I have loved you from the beginning. I will love you until the end. I love you and provide for you all the days of your life. Every day of your life has been ordained by me. You are my child; the child of the King. I have all you need. I AM all you need. I am the all-sufficient one, the Alpha and the Omega, the First and the Last, the Beginning and the End.

"But when he, the Spirit of truth, comes, he will guide you into all truth. He will not speak on his own; he will speak only what he hears, and he will tell you what is yet to come. He will bring glory to me by taking from what is mine and making it known to you. All that belongs to the Father is mine. That is why I said the Spirit will take from what is mine and make it known to you." (John 16:13-15)

The Holy Trinity

My precious child, I am the awesome triune God. It must be difficult for you to understand, but I AM. I am your Father in heaven. I knew you before I knit you together in your mother's womb. I am the Father of all creation. I am the master of the universe. All things exist because I ordered them into existence. I am the first person of the Trinity. I am the Most High God. I am the author and perfecter of all things seen and unseen. I am the Holy God Almighty. I am God, the Father.

My Son, Jesus Christ, is the Word. He was with me in the beginning. My Son and I are one. If you know my Son, you know me. If you have seen my Son, you have seen me. I sent my Son to save the world. He left his throne in heaven and became flesh. He was offered up as a sacrifice, the Lamb of God, to be the atonement for your sins. He has paid your ransom and bridged the distance that existed between you and me because of your sin.

My Son is the light of the world. He is the only way to me, God the Father. Jesus Christ is your eternal high priest. He pleads your case to me day and night. He has died to give you access to me, the holy of holies. You may approach my throne without fear and trembling because of the work of my Son. He is the propitiation for your sins. You have regained my favor because of his atoning sacrifice on the cross. Jesus has conquered death and the grave. He is the firstborn from the dead, and he returned to his throne in heaven on my right hand. Jesus Christ, my Son, is the second person in the Holy Trinity.

My Holy Spirit takes up residency in you and lives in your heart, when you confess Jesus as Lord, and believe that God raised him from the dead. The Holy Spirit is the third person in the Holy Trinity. Jesus sent the Holy Spirit to you, from me, to guide you into all truth. The

Spirit takes what is mine and makes it known to you. My Holy Spirit, your Counselor, speaks only what he hears from God the Father and God the Son. All that belongs to me will be made known to you through my Spirit.

My Spirit is my gift to you in Jesus' name. You have access to me 24/7 through my Spirit who lives in you. I know and see all things with the help of the Holy Spirit. You receive power through the Holy Spirit. You receive good gifts through the Spirit as he determines. Your body is the temple of God whose Spirit lives in you. The Spirit convicts the world of guilt in regard to sin and righteousness and judgment. The Spirit helps you in your weakness. He intercedes for you in accordance with my will. The Spirit, whom I put in your heart, is a deposit guaranteeing your inheritance of eternal life with me.

We are the great three-in-one God. We are God the Father, God the Son, and God the Holy Spirit. We are the Holy Trinity. I AM. Everything I have is available to you. My wisdom and my power I will share with you, by my Spirit, when you ask for it. My protection and my counsel are yours, by my Spirit, when you belong to me. Everything that Jesus taught on earth will be repeated to you by my Spirit. My healing, my comfort, and my peace are accessible by my Spirit, in Jesus' name. Forgiveness is freely given by me upon your asking. Knowledge and discernment I offer to you. A life of abundance is yours to receive when you live in me and walk by my Spirit.

You have no idea of the power, strength, and authority that is available to you by my Spirit who lives in your heart. Tap into this power by asking me. Allow my Spirit to guide your steps. Consult with the Spirit on all you do and say. Live in tune with my Spirit. Walk in his ways, and you walk with me. Live not by might, nor by power, but by my Spirit.

When Jesus spoke again to the people, he said, "I am the light of the world. Whoever follows me will never walk in darkness, but will have the light of life." (John 8:12)

Light of the World

I am the light of the world. When you follow me, you will never walk in darkness. My light is my truth. My bright light shines into the darkness and exposes all evil. The light of my life pierces the powers of this dark world. The truth of my light replaces every lie and deception the enemy presents.

When you walk with me, my light is a lamp unto your feet. The path I lay out for you is illuminated by my radiance. No shadow shall overtake you. I turn your darkness into light. My light makes everything more discernible. Things that were once not visible become detectable in the light. The invisible is now visible when you walk in my light.

Before I became a man and walked on the earth, you lived in darkness; but now that I am here, you have seen the light. I am the light, and my light is available to you. Do not fear the spirits of this dark world. I have overcome them, and I will overcome them again very soon. Remain in me, and I will remain in you. You have access to my power to overcome all forces of evil. You do not wage war as the world does. Your weapons have divine powers to demolish strongholds. When you live and walk in the light, there will be no darkness within you.

God made his light shine in your heart to give you the light of the knowledge of the glory of God in the face of Christ. I am the light. I am the glory of God. Look to me to see the glory of God. My life has brought glory to God, and God has glorified me in his presence. I am the light of the world. Walk with me, and walk in the truth. Follow me, and you will never walk in darkness again. Draw from my power, and you will surely overcome all evil.

He said: "The Lord is my rock, my fortress and my deliverer; my God is my rock, in whom I take refuge, my shield and the horn of my salvation. He is my stronghold, my refuge and my savior—from violent men you save me." (2 Samuel 22:2-3)

Your Rock and Your Refuge

I am your rock and your refuge. I am your stronghold in times of trouble. I am your fortress and your hiding place. When you are in danger, run to me, and I will protect you. As you face trial and tribulation, I will be your anchor of hope. Cling to me, and I will hold on to you. Have faith in me, and I will be your guide. You do not walk alone; I go with you wherever you go. When you face evil, I am on your side. Together we will stand and fight to overcome all forces against you.

Do not worry or be anxious about the future. Cast all your cares upon me, and I will sustain you. Give your burdens to me, and in return, I will give you rest. Trade in your anxiety for my perfect peace. A heart at peace gives life to the body. Bask in my peace, and experience true life as I have designed it. Slow down, breathe deeply, and rest in me. I will carry your load. A life too busy brings discontent. Eliminate the unnecessary, and concentrate on my will. I will show you the most excellent way.

Do not be lazy, but do not labor in vain only to store up a wealth of your own. Be generous with what you have. Give freely, as it has been given to you. Do not put your hope in wealth, which is uncertain; but put your hope in me, and I will provide you with everything for your enjoyment. I provide water for the thirsty. I provide food for the hungry. I provide rest for the weary and strength for the weak. I provide a way out, when there is no other way. I give you good gifts without cost. Trust in me, and I will supply you with all you require. Believe in me, and you will have a life that is full. I am your portion. I am all you need.

In the beginning was the Word, and the Word was with God, and the Word was God. He was with God in the beginning. (John 1:1)

The Word

I am the Word. I am God. I am the Word of God. I became flesh. I walked the earth as a man. I walked beside man. You say you would believe in me if you had walked with me, but I say when you believe in me, you will walk with me. I will send my Holy Spirit to dwell within you. You will be walking with me every moment of the day. You serve a risen and living God. A God who loves you so much, he makes your heart his dwelling; he lives inside you. How much closer can I be? How much more evidence do you need to believe in me?

You have direct access to my Word. My Holy Spirit will remind you of everything I have said. He will take what is mine, and make it known to you. Better yet, the Holy Spirit will personalize my Word for you. It's like you have your own personal version of my Word living inside you. You can ask me anything, at any time. I hear you, and I will answer you. You can receive my wisdom and my guidance whenever you desire it. My Counselor is your closest ally. My Comforter awaits your cry. Every tear you shed is felt by me. Every joy of yours is my joy first.

I am a lamp to your feet and a light for your path. My Word will direct you on your journey. Take it to heart and know my Word; it is sharper than any double-edged sword. My Word is the choicest of all weapons. Let my Word dwell within you. Know it and use it wisely. My Word is flawless. It is your shield of protection. My Word will conquer the greatest of enemies. My Word is truth. My Word exposes the darkness and brings it forth into the light.

I am the Word who lives among you and in you. Believe in my Word. I am the sacrificial Lamb of God by whom the world will receive its salvation. Believe in me, and you will be saved. Confess me as your Savior, and you will live forever. I am the Word of God. I AM.

"I am the vine; you are the branches. If a man remains in me and I in him, he will bear much fruit; apart from me you can do nothing." (John 15:5)

The True Vine

My Father sent me to do his will. I love my Father, so I do as he commands. If you love me, you will do as I command. Love me and love each other. Obey me, and remain in my love. Remain in me, and I will remain in you. You will not bear fruit on your own. You must remain in me.

My Father, the gardener, trims the branches that do not bear fruit, so that they do not take life away from those which are bearing fruit. Do not be found unfruitful, but love each other as I have loved you. How have I loved you? I laid down my life for you. Love sacrificially. Love unconditionally. Love obediently. There is no greater love than this.

Can a branch bear fruit apart from the vine? I tell you it is not possible. Can you grow in your love when you are not in me? This, too, is not possible. You must remain in me. How do you remain in me? Listen to my teaching. Obey my commands. Tune into my Spirit. Take your instruction from me. Follow my example. Live as I have lived. Love as I have loved. Enter the narrow gate that leads to life—not just life, but life eternal.

Vine-ripened fruits taste better than other fruits because they stay on the vine longer. Remain in the vine and bear the choicest of fruits. Remain in me, and eat of the Tree of Life. There is no better fruit than the fruit of life everlasting. Linger in my presence. Wait upon me. Seek me with all your heart. Know my ways. Incline your ear to my teaching. Listen to the voice of the Spirit. Meet with me away from the noise, and experience all I have to give you. Time spent with me will not be unproductive. Live a fruit-bearing life in me. Others will know me by your fruit. Others will be brought to a life of salvation because you cared enough to bear the fruit of my love. Remain in me. I am the true vine.

Now may the Lord of peace himself give you peace at all times and in every way. The Lord be with all of you. (2 Thessalonians 3:16)

Prince of Peace

Peace I give you, for I am the Prince of Peace. I am always with you. I am the peace you need. Your world is so busy. Your time is all tied up. You have so little time for me, but when you remain in me, I will give you peace. Spend time with me away from the noise and activity. I will give you peace during your most stressful times. My peace is accompanied by confidence and joy—the confidence of knowing that I am in control, and the joy of knowing that I love you and take care of you.

When your day is planned from start to finish with no room for me, it may feel to you as if I am not with you, but I am. I walk with you every step of the way. I wait patiently for you to seek me. When you rush ahead in the plans you have made for yourself, sometimes you feel unappreciated and empty by the end of the day. I would fill you up with my Spirit, if only you would ask. When you know me, there is no reason to feel empty. I am here. I love you. I appreciate you. I want to spend time with you. I want to replace your stress with a calm spirit. I want to fill you with my love. I want to cover you with my joy and peace.

Be confident in knowing that I am in control. Leave room in your day for me. Allow me to map out your time. Your prosperity is very important to me. You can live a good life without me, but will it be my best for you? My ways are higher than your ways. I know what is best for you. Will you trust me to lead you in that direction, even when it may not be consistent with your plans? Cast all your anxieties on me. I will give you rest. Rest in my arms, and allow me to carry you down this road you are on. I will build you up, and when I set you down, you will run in the confidence of my commands. I know the plans I have for you. My peace is inlaid in the steps I have marked out for you. Go in the peace I designed for you.

And so we know and rely on the love God has for us. God is love. Whoever lives in love lives in God, and God in him. (1 John 4:16)

God is Love

I am love. I am the perfect example of love. My love is so great that I gave up my own Son for you. I sent my only Son to the world to save the world. I asked him to give his life in exchange for yours. He was the sacrificial Lamb of God. He willingly obeyed me. He suffered death on a cross so that you would be reconciled to me. He has paid the price for your iniquities, and made you my adopted daughter. You are my child whom I love.

Your love comes from me. You are able to love because you know me. Love one another with my love. Love another unconditionally. Love your brother whether you feel like it or not. You have the capacity to love because I loved you first. When you love others, it is apparent that you live in me, and I live in you. My love is made complete in you. You must testify of my love. Testify to the sacrifice I made on your behalf. Let others see my love through you. Let others know where your love comes from. Love in action and in truth, not with words.

You need not fear because you are loved. Perfect love drives out all fear. My love is made complete in you, so that you may remain confident on the Day of Judgment, because you are like me. You believe in me, so you have a place in my eternal kingdom. When you love me, you will carry out my commands. Your will is obedient to my will. Your life is not your own. You belong to me. Let your love shine like a light in the darkness. You will be a beacon for all to see and know that I am God. Love gives way to greater love.

I am love. I love you, my precious child. I love you so that you, in turn, may love another. Experience me, and you will experience my love. Without love, you are nothing; you gain nothing. Love is the most excellent way. Love never fails. My love never fails you. You have the most excellent gift I have to give you, my love. Love me first, and love others as I love you.

"But the Counselor, the Holy Spirit, whom the Father will send in my name, will teach you all things and will remind you of everything I have said to you." (John 14:26)

Counselor

I am your Counselor. I am the Holy Spirit whom the Father sends to live inside you when you believe in Jesus as your Savior and Lord. I am God in you. Can you even understand that? You do not worship a god that is dead or made of stone. You worship a living God who makes his home inside you. You have access to God all the time. God is with you all the time. I am God with you.

I do not speak of my own volition, but only what I hear from God the Father and God the Son. I will guide you into the truth. I will testify about Jesus. I will remind you of what Jesus said to you. I will teach you all things. The world will condemn you, but you are not condemned. The father of lies will try to deceive you; but I will expose him, and bring him into the light. Seek me for discernment. I am the Spirit of truth. I am the gift of God who leads you to the throne of him who saves you. I intercede for you.

Do you need comfort? I am your Comforter. Do you need wisdom? God's wisdom I carry with me at all times. Do you need respite? Rest in me. I am your refuge. Do you need healing? I offer you God's healing touch. Do you need companionship? I will stick closer than a friend to you. Do you need compassion? I understand what you are going through. I care about you.

Listen to my voice. When you hear me, you hear God. My counsel is God's will for you. I know my Father's will. You know my Father, and you know me. I live to please God. I will speak only what God tells me. I will teach only what Jesus taught. I have your best interest in mind. My home is in your heart. Are you at home with me? I am at home with you. Let's spend time together. What a wonderful gift God gave you in the Spirit. I am with you always.

"All the prophets testify about him that everyone who believes in him receives forgiveness of sins through his name." (Acts 10:43)

Forgiver

Do you believe in me? When you confess your sins and believe in me, you are forgiven. Your sins have been pardoned. You have been excused from the death sentence. The wages of sin is death, but I paid your debt on the cross. You have been exonerated in my name. Your slate has been wiped clean. I have blotted out all your transgressions. The great chasm that once separated you from God has been bridged by my obedience to God's will, even unto death.

I died so that you would be forgiven and reconciled to your heavenly Father. Now you must also forgive those who trespass against you. Your debt was great, but it has been paid. Forgive the debts of those who sin against you; and your heavenly Father will forgive you; but when you do not forgive men their sins, your Father in heaven will not forgive you of your sins. How many times have I forgiven you? In turn, you must forgive your brother time and time again. If you forgive anyone, my Father also forgives him.

In me you have redemption. You have been delivered from your sins. Do not be bound by sin and temptation. Repent of your sin and be free from all temptation, for I will provide the way out. Find your freedom in me. Turn away from your wicked ways, and become the new creature I have designed you to be. Your sins have been forgiven. You have been washed clean. You will trade in your filthy rags for my robe of righteousness.

I love you so much that I laid my life down for yours. You are my child, my beloved bride. You are now without spot or blemish. You have been made clean in my name. Forgive others as you have been forgiven. Do not hold onto the sins that have already been forgiven in my name. Let go of the misdeeds from your past, and find freedom in my forgiveness.

"Salvation is found in no one else, for there is no other name under heaven given to men by which we must be saved." (Acts 4:12)

Savior

I am the Lord. Apart from me there is no savior. No one comes to the Father except by me. My life was given as a ransom for your sin. I have paid your debt—the wages of your sin is death. The Father sent me to die in your place. I died for your sin. You are saved because of God's great mercy, not because of anything you have done.

You have been released from the burden of guilt. I rescued you from a certain destiny to the eternal lake of fire. I delivered you from evil. When you believe in me, believe that I died for your sin, believe that God raised me from the dead, and you will be saved. Confess with your mouth that I am Lord, and you will receive the gift of eternal life from God the Father.

I am your protector. I guard you from your attacker. I am your strength and your shield. I clothe you in my armor, and I defend you against your enemy all day long. I send you my angels, and give them charge over you. You are never out of my sight. You are never out of my reach. I am with you always. You may put your hope and trust in me. I am dependable. I am trustworthy.

I am your Redeemer. I traded my life for yours. I redeemed your life by suffering and dying in your place. I took on the punishment for your sin. Your debt has been paid. You have been given a second chance at life—even life eternal. I died for you—will you now live for me? Let my light shine through you. Think of me. Remain in me. Let all you say and do be done for the glory of God. I am the God who saved you. I am your Savior and your Lord.

He heals the brokenhearted and binds up their wounds. (Psalm 147:3)

Healer and Restorer

Your heart has been broken, but I am here. I will bind up your wounds one by one. I will restore your heart to a more healthy state. It will be even stronger than it was before. Allow me to touch you; I will rebuild you. Receive the healing that I have to give you. Have faith in the one who created you.

You have suffered great loss, but I am with you. The devastation that you have experienced will soon come to an end. I will preserve you and restore your soul. I will provide for you. I care deeply for you. My compassions do not fail. My mercies are new every morning. Cast your burdens and your cares upon me. I will give you a lighter load to carry. I will rebuild you and give you a new start.

You have been stricken with illness, but I am your healer. Your diseases and infirmities are not too great for me. I will restore you to good health. I will take away your afflictions, and bring healing to your body. I will anoint you with the oil of healing, and bring restoration and joy to your soul.

You have an addiction that rules your life, but I am in control. No bondage is too strong for me to break. I will cut you loose from your captor. I will hem you in, and protect you from yourself. I will strengthen your will, and empower you to overcome your compulsion. Depend on me alone. I will pull you through. Together we will defeat the spirits of darkness.

You need a healer; I am the one you seek. Come to me. Find your rest in my arms. Let my peace permeate your soul. Let me rejoice over you with singing. Let me quiet you with my love. My healing touch will restore your brokenness. Lean on me. I am here.

It is because of him that you are in Christ Jesus, who has become for us wisdom from God—that is, our righteousness, holiness and redemption. (1 Corinthians 1:30)

Wisdom of God

I am wisdom from God. The wisdom of the wise has been destroyed. The wisdom of the world has been made foolishness. In the wisdom and power of God, I have come to save the world. You are not considered wise by the world's standards. Your belief in me may give you the label of the foolish one in this world, but I have overcome the world. The foolish will shame the wise. Do not speak of the wisdom of this age, but of God's secret wisdom and power.

You have the Spirit of wisdom within you. The Spirit of God, who dwells within you, knows the thoughts of God and makes them known to you. You will, therefore, speak words not of human wisdom, but of God's wisdom taught to you by his Spirit. Because the Spirit of God lives within you, you have the mind of Christ. You have spiritual wisdom and discernment because the Spirit of God is in you. You may know and understand the things of God because you have been given the Spirit of God.

God has made foolish the wisdom of the world. You were born of the world and taught the wisdom of the world. Now, you are born again with the Spirit of the Lord; and therefore, possess the wisdom of God. God's wisdom is supreme. Get wisdom and understanding though it may cost you all you have.

Wisdom will protect you and guide you on straight paths. I am the wisdom of God. I will protect you and guide you. My Spirit lives within you. You have access to the wisdom of God at all times. Listen to my words with all your heart; I give you sound learning. Do not forsake my teaching. Keep my commands, and live in the wisdom that God has given you.

We have this hope as an anchor for the soul, firm and secure. It enters the inner sanctuary behind the curtain, where Jesus, who went before us, has entered on our behalf. He has become a high priest forever, in the order of Melchizedek. (Hebrews 6:19-20)

High Priest

I am the high priest appointed by God Most High. In reverent submission, I came to do the will of God. I have offered my body as a living sacrifice once for all. No longer is it necessary for high priests to offer sacrifices and offerings as atonement for your sin. You have been made holy through the sacrifice of my body on the cross. Your hope is secure in me. Your soul has been saved by me.

Daily I offer up prayers and petitions on your behalf. I live to intercede for you every day at the throne of God. Without the shedding of blood there is no forgiveness, but I have freed you from your sin by pouring out my own blood for you. I have made you to be a kingdom and priest to serve my God and Father. You are chosen by me, to be a priest of God, and declare the praises of him who called you out of darkness into his wonderful light. Share the good news of my death and resurrection with all peoples of the earth.

I have taken my place with God in heaven. I am seated at his right hand. Because of God's great love for you, and by his grace, you are saved. He has raised you up with me, and seated you with me in the heavenly realm. He has adopted you as his daughter, in accordance with his pleasure and will. You will spend eternity with us in the heavenly place.

I am your great high priest. I have given myself as a sacrifice for your sin. The veil of the temple was torn. You now have full access to God. You may enter the holy of holies, and approach his throne in freedom and with confidence. God, our Father, hears your requests and listens to your cries. He answers them one by one. He knows every intimate detail of your life by his Spirit who lives inside you. Listen to the Spirit. Know and do his will.

It shone with the glory of God, and its brilliance was like that of a very precious jewel, like a jasper, clear as crystal. (Revelation 21:11)

Like a Diamond

Like a flawless diamond, the most precious of all the jewels I made, I am multifaceted. My character consists of many qualities. Like a diamond, light bounces off every surface of my being. I am flawless, a perfect prism reflecting my own beauty. Let me help you experience some facets of my nature.

I am truthful. I speak the truth. You will find no dishonesty within me. I am sincere. My truth pierces through the darkness like a sword, exposing all lies and insincerities. I am the truth.

I am genuine. I am the real deal—an authentic God. There is no falsehood in me. I am not a fake or an imitation. I am what I say I am. I do what I say I will do. I have integrity. I am not an idol or statue to worship. I am the same yesterday, today, and forever.

I am faithful. I am reliable and dependable. You can believe in me. You can count on me. I will come through for you. I keep my promises. I will not let you down. You are important to me. I keep my covenant of love to those who love me, and keep my commands.

I am trustworthy. Put your hope and trust in me. Be confident in my commitment to you. I am constant and consistent. I am honorable and upright. I care for those who trust in me. Blessed are you when you put your trust in the name of the Lord.

I am great and powerful. There is no limit to my capacity. I have authority over all the earth. My strength and my might are more awesome than you can comprehend. I am a supreme force. Nothing is too hard for me. I have overcome the spirits of darkness. I would love to display my power in you. My power is made perfect in your weakness.

I possess all the brilliance of a rare jewel. I am a precious gem. My beauty is reflected in my substance. My character is flawless. I am like a diamond, the most precious of stones.

.

Chapter 7

REMAIN IN ME

*In good times and bad,
we remain faithful and steadfast,
and God will lead us through.*

When times are good, be happy; but when times are bad, consider: God has made the one as well as the other. (Ecclesiastes 7:14)

In Good Times and Bad Times

Rejoice in the good times; be thankful in the bad. I have made them all. Your happiness should not be dependent upon enjoying good times alone. I have fashioned hard times for you to endure as well. I do not give you difficulty to watch you toil. I do not take pleasure in your pain. I allow you to struggle at times because suffering produces perseverance. Growth in your character and spiritual maturity are achieved by walking through the valleys and climbing the mountains in front of you. I am willing to allow you to bear this challenge for your own good.

Remember, you are not alone. I am with you always. Call on me anytime of the day or night. I am by your side. I do not expect that you suffer alone. I do not desire that you find your own way through the thicket. I allow the bad times, so that you will run to me. Allow me to walk with you through the fire. I am your spiritual guide. I would never ask you to do what I have not already done myself. Admit your vulnerability. Seek me for your strength. When you are weak; you are strong. My power is made perfect in your weakness.

Delight in hardships. Celebrate adversity. Be happy in good times and bad. It is to your benefit to acquire my wisdom as you persevere through your trials. The wisdom you gain will preserve your life. Search for it as buried treasure. Cherish it as a precious jewel. Your trouble will be over soon, and you will be all the better for it. Rich is the man who gains his wealth in wisdom. The fool is the one who despises my wisdom. Next time you face a giant on your path, rely on me as you confront it. I will be your strength. We will slay the giant together, and celebrate the victory of the battle.

"I have told you these things, so that in me you may have peace. In this world you will have trouble. But take heart! I have overcome the world." (John 16:33)

I Have Overcome the World

Do you think that because you believe in me, there will be no trouble in your life? I would love to spare you from all your pain, but you live in a fallen world. There is too much sin and strife in my kingdom on earth. That is not what I had hoped for. When I gave man and woman the gift of free will, my expectations were greater—but mankind has chosen another way. I gave humans dominion over the earth I created and all that is in it. How do you think they are doing?

The sin of man has desecrated what I so carefully designed, but I will not take away the gift of your free will or your authority over what I have given you. There is trouble in your life because of the world man has created for himself. I will walk with you through your trials. I will always protect you, and at times, I will save you; but if I were to rescue you from all your troubles, how would you acquire my wisdom? Where would you find my discernment? When would you realize your dependence on me?

Though your troubles seem monumental and long-suffering to you, they are but a fleck in the landscape of time. You will experience trials and tribulations in this world, but take heart! I have overcome the world. I have conquered sin and death. I have been resurrected to new life. I sit on the throne at the right hand of my Father. He has made me Lord of all. A time is coming when I will return to the earth. The kingdom of this world will become my kingdom, and I will reign on high forever. My enemies will be made my footstool. When this time comes, you will experience a trouble-free life in eternity with me. Until then, accept the peace I have to give you. You have the peace of knowing you belong to me, and better times lie ahead. Anchor yourself in the hope of eternity. Rest assured that I have overcome the world!

So do not fear, for I am with you; do not be dismayed, for I am your God. I will strengthen you and help you; I will uphold you with my righteous right hand. (Isaiah 41:10)

I Will Strengthen You

When you are weak, it is then you are strong. When you are vulnerable, my strength in you becomes visible. My power is made perfect in weakness. When you agree you cannot do it on your own, call on my name; I will step in and do it with you. When you give yourself fully to me, I can accomplish so much more than when you attempt to maintain some control.

Whatever you set your mind to, do it with your whole heart. Complete your tasks as if you are working for me. Honor me with your diligence. Glorify me with your service. In your obedience, I will reward you with my everlasting joy. I have begun a good work in you, and I will carry it on to completion. You are being transformed daily into the likeness of Christ.

Submit yourself to me fully, and let me do my work in you. Present yourself to me, and I will arm you with my strength. Nothing is impossible with me. Yield your heart to my Spirit, and bear the fruit of the same. Live by the Spirit, and the fruit of my love will shine from your face. Stay in step with the Spirit, and my peace will belong to you.

You can do anything I ask you to do. I will give you the strength to move mountains. Great armies will fall at your feet. Surrender your heart and mind to my leading. I am the one who will guide and protect you. Listen to my voice in the still of the night, and I will lead you home. My way is marked out for you; I implore you to walk in it. I am the force behind your initiative. I give you the passion for the tasks I assign you. I equip you with the tools you require. You will lack nothing when you remain in me.

There is nothing you cannot do when you set your mind on the things above. Run into the wind with nothing to fear. I am your driving force. I am your stronghold. I will shadow you with my wings. You will not grow weary. Remain in me, and find your strength in me.

It is for freedom that Christ has set us free. Stand firm, then, and do not let yourselves be burdened again by a yoke of slavery. (Galatians 5:1)

I Have Set You Free

At one time you were held in captivity, bound by the chains around your neck. You were a prisoner of the enemy who seeks to destroy you because you are mine. You once were enslaved by the thoughts my adversary forced upon you. Behold, I came to release you from your bondage. It is for freedom that I have set you free. Do not take upon yourself the opponent's yoke of slavery again. I have overcome the enemy of your soul. I declare the victory in the battle for your heart. You are my child; you belong to me.

Once you walked in darkness, but now you have seen the light. I am the light of the world shining before all men. I pierce the darkness with my sword. The darkness gives way to the light. I am the truth, and the truth shall set you free. I have revealed the deceitful ways of your captor. Never again should you live within the prison walls he sets up before you. You have tasted the sweetness of liberty. Be wise. Do not forget the one who has set you free.

I will not render you helpless. You hold my power in your hands. Remain alert, and prepare for the battle. Know my Word, and use it as your weapon. It will stop your enemy in his tracks. Nothing can penetrate like the Word of God. Put on my suit of armor; it will protect your heart and mind. Worship me in gladness, and ward away all evil.

Remember it is for freedom that I have set you free. Protect yourself from the slavery of sin. Do not return to your former ways. You are a new creation. The old has passed away, and the new is yet to come. Walk in the narrow way, and do not depart from it. Keep your focus on the prize I have set before you, and do not look back. Live in the freedom I have provided for you. It did not come without a price. I paid it willingly for your sake. Remain in me, and maintain the liberation of your soul.

"I am the vine; you are the branches. If a man remains in me and I in him, he will bear much fruit; apart from me you can do nothing." (John 15:5)

Remain in Me

My beloved children, you are not the grapes, the fruit of the vine. Nor are you the vine. I am the vine; you are the branches. Remain in me, and I will remain in you. When you remain in me, you will find life in me. Apart from me, you can do nothing—you will bear no fruit. Remain in me, and you will produce fruit in my kingdom. A dead or dying branch will bear no fruit. Therefore, live life with a heart that is fully alive in me. You will be fruitful.

When you remain in me, and find your life in me, my Spirit remains in you. The Spirit gives you life. No longer will you be dead in your sin, gratifying your old nature, but you will be alive by the Spirit. Your new life in me will display the fruit of the Spirit. The fruit the Spirit produces in you is: love, joy, peace, patience, kindness, goodness, faithfulness, gentleness, and self-control. When others see the fruit of the vine, they will desire a life like yours. Your life in the vine will produce fruit in yourself and fruit in my kingdom.

The fruit you produce in my kingdom will be the person who witnesses your life with me, and desires a similar relationship with the vine. You will be fruitful when others see my goodness in you. My goodness in you can be seen only when you remain close to me, and live by the Spirit. Stay in the vine. Outside of relationship with me, your life does not appear inviting; it seems no different than any other life. The branch receives its life from the vine. You are alive in me.

Do not cut yourself off from the vine. Do not be an outsider, but maintain an intimate relationship with the one who created you and gives you life in the fullest. Cling to me, and I will hold on to you. I gave my life as a ransom for yours. Was my death pointless? Apart from me, your witness will be ineffective. Live your life in me, and take notice of the fruit of the Spirit, which will, in turn, produce fruit in my kingdom.

"Everyone will be salted with fire. Salt is good, but if it loses its saltiness, how can you make it salty again? Have salt in yourselves, and be at peace with each other." (Mark 9:49)

The Fire within You

My child, I am so pleased that you want to keep the flame of passion for me burning within you. Let me be the fuel for your fire. You know how I feel about lukewarm Christians. I will chew them up and spit them out of my mouth. Your desire to live with a heart fully alive is my desire for you, too. How do you keep your heart alive? Live by the Spirit. The Spirit will bring more salt and fire to your life than you could ever imagine.

Salt is the seasoning of a life in me. Do not lose your saltiness or let your flame die out. Spend time with me. I will salt you with the fire of refinement. Keep yourself salty by being in tune with my Holy Spirit living inside you. Do not grieve the Spirit, but let the Spirit of truth guide you in all truth. Listen to his instruction. When you are obedient to me, you will experience great joy, unlike mere happiness that the world promises. My joy overflowing in you adds spice to your life. Others will taste and see that I am good.

Your Counselor, the Spirit, will teach you all things, and remind you of everything I have said to you. He will take from me what is mine, and make it known to you. All that belongs to the Father is mine, and therefore, it is yours too. Salt yourself with the Spirit. This must be accomplished on a daily basis, or you will most assuredly lose your saltiness. Do not forsake meeting with me. Remain in me, and I will remain in you. My salt is your spice for life. Live your life fully alive in me. There is no more excellent way.

When you have salt in yourself, you will experience a life of peace. Life in the Spirit produces a confidence that others do not comprehend. Being confident in your faith produces confidence in your present life and in your future. There is no greater peace than knowing your future is secure with me. Be at peace with each other because you are salted by me.

Therefore, since we are surrounded by such a great cloud of witnesses, let us throw off everything that hinders and the sin that so easily entangles, and let us run with perseverance the race marked out for us. Let us fix our eyes on Jesus, the author and perfecter of our faith, who for the joy set before him endured the cross, scorning its shame, and sat down at the right hand of the throne of God. Consider him who endured such opposition from sinful men, so that you will not grow weary and lose heart. (Hebrews 12:1-3)

Persevere

My love, do not grow weary and lose heart. Your opponent loves to busy up your life so that you do not have time or energy for me. Do not take on too many "good" things, but seek me to know my "best" for you. The enemy's mission is to hinder you from me. He enjoys presenting you with great opportunities that will exhaust your time. He loves to tie you up in bondage to sin, and then accuse you and shame you into his submission. Be alert! I have already won this battle. You are victorious in Jesus Christ.

My Son endured death on a cross to pay for your sin and bail you out of your destination to eternal damnation. Do not lose sight of what Jesus has already done for you. Press on toward the goal. I have marked out a race for you. Your finish line is marked by the gates of heaven. Run with perseverance. Do not let the enemy cut in on you, and distract you from achieving your goal of eternity with me. I hold the stopwatch. I govern this race.

Fix your eyes on me alone. Run toward me, and do not look back. Do not step to the left or to the right. Placing your foot on another path that I have not cleared for you may cause you to stumble and fall. Be steadfast in your commitment to me. Your dedication will reward you one hundred-fold. My blessings are abundant for the unwavering, faithful one. Celebrate your victory in me! The race has been won. You will spend eternity with me in the place I have prepared for you. Persevere and stay on track. Do not grow weary and lose heart. Continue in the right direction, and your inheritance from the Lord will be your reward.

Two are better than one, because they have a good return for their work: If one falls down, his friend can help him up. But pity the man who falls and has no one to help him up! (Ecclesiastes 4:9-10)

Two are Better than One

My child, I am so happy that you come to me when you feel overwhelmed by life. You do not have the energy or the frame of mind you need to accomplish your tasks today? Your head is clouded, and you are not able to focus on your work? Do not feel overcome with shame and sadness at your present state. Shame is from the evil one. When you are not able to begin or accomplish what you have set out to do, it may be because you attempt it alone.

When you do not spend time with me first, you start off on the wrong foot, but now, you have come to the right place. I am your source of life. You will do all things by my strength. On your own, you may not accomplish as much, but with me, together we will do great things. Two are better than one. You will have a better return for your work when you are yoked with me. If you fall down, I am there to pick you up. Join yourself with me.

My beloved one, you are good because you are mine. My "to-do" list for you will not overwhelm you. You have only one thing to do today—spend time with me. Seek me, tell me, listen to me, follow me, and rest in me. That is all I have for you to accomplish today. The remainder of the day will take care of itself. There is a time to work and a time to have fun. There is a time to plant and a time to reap. There is a time to be busy and a time to be still. There is a time for everything under heaven.

Today, you will be still and rest in me. My yoke is easy and my burden is light. Partner with me today. Two are better than one. We will accomplish much more together than you could ever accomplish on your own. Step forward first with your right foot as I step forward with mine; your left foot will follow. My steps are not too big for you. Put one foot in front of the other in the path I map out for you. As we walk it together, everything else will fall into order. Should you stumble, you will not fall, for I am here to help you. I give you my hand.

Find satisfaction in your work today. Take delight in what you set your hands to do. No task is too large; no task is too meaningless, but all work done with me by your side is toil worth the effort. To those who please me, I give wisdom, knowledge, and happiness. You are pleasing to me because you have taken time for me today. Be at ease with your life, and leave your worries to me. You are not alone; you are with me, and two are better than one.

"This is the covenant I will make with them after that time, says the Lord. I will put my laws in their hearts, and I will write them on their minds." Then he adds: "Their sins and lawless acts I will remember no more." And where these have been forgiven, there is no longer any sacrifice for sin. (Hebrews 10:16-18)

Divine Dementia

I have chosen to forget your ways. I no longer remember your sins and lawlessness. You have been forgiven. Your debt was paid at the cross. I replace the evil devices in your heart and mind with my laws and commandments. This is my promise to you. You have been forgiven. You are my child. You belong to me. You will not suffer the sacrifice for your sin. Jesus paid the ultimate price on the cross—once for all—once for you. You have been redeemed. You are a new creation in Christ Jesus. The old is gone, the new is here.

Now you must choose the same. Forget your old ways. Do not torment yourself with memories of your past sin. I have wiped clean your slate. There is no room for shame when your heart has been redeemed by me. I release you from your guilt. I free you from your disgrace. I have replaced your remorse with honor and righteousness. You are justified by my grace. Your name is written in the book of life. You will spend eternity with me.

Your obedience is my joy. Remember my laws. I have written them on your mind. I have put them in your heart. Abide by them. Your life will be long and prosperous. You will experience the joy of my salvation when you conform to my ways. Listen for my voice in your heart. You know my voice. Act upon my directions. I have mapped out the best possible road for you to travel upon. I will not lead you astray. Be willing to change your course when necessary. I know what is in your best interest. I will prosper you. You will live a full life in the abundance I have planned for you. Delight yourself in me. I give you the desires of your heart. Stay close to me. I will never leave your side. Trust me with your life. You may depend on me. I will provide all that you ever need. Remain in me, and I will remain in you.

The Sovereign Lord has given me an instructed tongue, to know the word that sustains the weary. He wakens me morning by morning, wakens my ear to listen like one being taught. The Sovereign Lord has opened my ears, and I have not been rebellious; I have not drawn back. (Isaiah 50:4-5)

Listen to My Voice

Good morning, my faithful one. Do you hear me calling? Wake up, my child. It's time for our daily conversation. I have opened your ears; they are ready to listen. I will teach you so many things today. Do not roll over and return to your slumber. Do not replace me with a less vital activity. I am here to listen to you and speak to you. There is an abundance of instruction on my lips for you today. Trust me. I have your best interests in mind.

You carry heavy burdens today. Do not go it alone. I am here to shift the weight of your worries onto my back. I have a lighter load for you to bear. Join me in my yoke today. I will not lead you astray. Follow in my footsteps. I will lead you down paths of righteousness. We will walk side-by-side to your destination. When the road is rough, I am here to carry you. I will lead you to greener pastures—an oasis in your desert.

Listen to my voice. Hear what I have to say to you today. You are my precious child. I love you more than you will ever understand. I want the best in life for you. I have significant assignments for you to carry out in advancing my kingdom. Your troubles seem enormous to you. I understand that, but I see the grander picture. Your afflictions are a momentary inconvenience on the journey I have laid out for you. I would not allow you to suffer these trials without using them for my good. Stay alert. There are many lessons to be learned from these encumbrances. You will be a better person on the other side of this valley.

Amidst the static and noise of your problems, listen for my voice. Hear my appraisal of the situation. Heed my warnings. Obey my instructions. I will lead you out. You are my prized possession. I will not let you perish. Cling to me; I am your Savior and Lord.

But who can endure the day of his coming? Who can stand when he appears? For he will be like a refiner's fire or a launderer's soap. (Malachi 3:2)

Whiter Than Snow

I am coming again. Are you ready? Have you made the effort to cultivate a life of clean living? Have you shed the dirt of the sin I found you in? Have you turned over a new leaf and left behind your former ways? Do you remain in your sin or have you turned your back on it? Do you resist the devil? Are you aware of his schemes? Does he hold you in his grip? Have you experienced the freedom of my forgiveness, or do you cling to the chains of your guilt and shame?

Get up! Come to me. Believe in my name. Confess me as your Savior. Accept my gift of grace. I will forgive all your sins. I will cleanse you from all unrighteousness. I will wash you whiter than snow. I will wipe your slate clean and renew your heart. I will cleanse you from the impurities in your soul. My fire of refinement will polish your character. I will make you a new creature. Your sinful life will be abolished and replaced by a new life of virtue.

You are my child, the one I love so dearly. When I come again, you will experience the gift of eternal life, your inheritance in full. When I return, you will stand before me. The name on your forehead will say: "Redeemed." I will accept you into my heavenly home, and give you the place I have prepared for you. We will live together in a time without end.

You are a new creation. You have been polished with the fire of refinement. Stand before me in the robe I have clothed you in. You are my child—the heir of my kingdom. All that I have is yours. All that I am I give to you. I have made you in my image. Live out the life I have called you to. Remain pure until I return again. Stand firm in your faith. Do not waver. Be a light shining in a dark world. Testify to the truth about me. I am the Savior of the world, and I will come again in the clouds. Will you be ready? Who will stand with you?

My dwelling place will be with them; I will be their God, and they will be my people. (Ezekiel 37:27)

My Home in You

Honey, I'm home. I declare my dwelling place in you. Not only do I live with you, I live within you. My Spirit resides in your heart. You have access to me 24/7. I am not going anywhere. The very moment you accepted Jesus as your Savior, I sent my Spirit to live inside you. That is my gift to you. I am your God. You are my child. You have this kind of connection with me because of the sacrifice of my Son. The veil of the temple was torn when he died on the cross for your sins. You have been reconciled to me, and now my Spirit lives inside you.

Do you understand what this means? Really? I, the one and only true God of the universe, have chosen you for my temple. My Spirit is within you. You have access to my heart and mind, at all times, as I relate myself to you by my Holy Spirit. You can draw on my strength for all things. You may hear my voice anytime you choose to listen. You are made in my image for my glory. You walk in the presence of your Creator. I created you to love you, and now I make my home in you. You are my own.

Remain in me, and I will remain in you. Make our relationship your first priority. Seek me first in all you do. I am only a whisper away. Speak to me anytime, and I will answer. Call on me day and night. I am here for you. Make me the captain of your ship, and I will steer you in the right direction. Keep my Word in your heart and mind, so you may draw on it in your hour of need. Protect yourself from the evil one. Do not strike your foot against a rock or cause your brother to stumble. Do not stray far from me. I will draw you back into the fold with my staff. You are my sheep, and I am your shepherd. I will take care of you.

The righteous cry out, and the Lord hears them; he delivers them from all their troubles. The Lord is close to the brokenhearted and saves those who are crushed in spirit. A righteous man may have many troubles, but the Lord delivers him from them all; he protects all his bones, not one of them will be broken. (Psalm 34:17-20)

I Will Deliver You

I hear you, my righteous child. I hear your cries in the midst of your troubles. I will deliver you from every one. Even the righteous will endure trials and suffering. There is no escaping afflictions and strife just because you know me. Your trials and tribulations may be many in this world, but I will rescue you from them all. At times, it is in your best interest that I allow you to experience trouble, but I will never leave you to deal with it on your own. I am always by your side. I will see you through. When the road is too rocky, I will even carry you.

Has your heart been broken? I will stay close to you. You may lean on me when your legs will no longer support you. I have been in your shoes. I have carried burdens too heavy to bear. I have experienced the pain of disappointment. My heart has been broken by the ones I love. I know your pain. I will see you through this difficult time, and set your feet on solid ground. Now place your feet on top of mine, and I will lead you to brighter days.

Has your spirit been crushed? Has the wind been removed from your sails? I know the ache your heart suffers. I was crushed for your iniquities. I carried the weight of your sins and bore the pain of your transgressions through my death on the cross, but I am alive again. My Spirit lives in you. I will save you from your anguish. I will lift you up out of the pit. My Spirit will take hold of yours, and show you to greater heights. I will remove the weight that holds you down, and give you a lighter load to carry.

I hear your cries. The rain falls on both the righteous and the unrighteous. In this world there will be trouble, even for those who believe in my name; but I have overcome the world, and seen the light of life. I will deliver you, so that you may experience the same light.

"As the Father has loved me, so have I loved you. Now remain in my love. If you obey my commands, you will remain in my love, just as I have obeyed my Father's commands and remain in his love." (John 15:9-10)

Remain in My Love

My beloved child, I love you as the Father loves me. You will remain in my love when you obey my commands. I have been obedient to my Father's commands, and my Father loves me still. I willingly obeyed my Father as I went to the cross to die for you—obedient unto death. Love each other the way I have loved you; and you will remain in my love. Be willing to lay down your life for your friend, as I have laid down my life for you. You are my friend. All that is my Father's belongs to me, and I will give you all I have.

If you do not obey my teaching, you do not love me. If you love me, you will listen to what I have taught you and act on it. This is the greatest lesson I have taught you: Love God with all your heart, soul, mind, and strength, and love each other as I have loved you. When you obey me, you remain in my love. My Father will love you, and we will make our home in you. My Father will send you the Holy Spirit, and he will remind you of what I have said.

If you love me, my Father will love you. I will love you, and show myself to you. You will see me in the Spirit I have given you. I am in my Father, and my Father is in me. The Spirit is in both of us, and we are in the Spirit. The Spirit that lives in you is the Spirit of God. Do you really grasp the meaning of all of this? The Father and I are one. You and I are one. You are one in the Spirit, and the Spirit is one in us. This is the greatest mystery of all. Do not try to figure it all out. It is much more than your mind can handle. Keep in tune with the Spirit inside you. He will guide you into all wisdom. Leave the big stuff to me. Just do as I do, and remain in my love. I have always loved you, and I love you still.

Who shall separate us from the love of Christ? Shall trouble or hardship or persecution or famine or nakedness or danger or sword? As it is written: "For your sake we face death all day long; we are considered as sheep to be slaughtered." No, in all these things we are more than conquerors through him who loved us. (Romans 8:35-37)

More than Conquerors

You are the child I adore. You are dearly loved by me. You have been called according to my purpose. I have given my own Son for you—his life in exchange for yours. I am the giver of all good gifts. I graciously give you all that belongs to me. Even so, there will be tough times ahead. You will face many challenges, but you will be triumphant in all circumstances because I am by your side. You have nothing to fear.

There will be persecution in the days ahead. You will be challenged for your allegiance to me, but you will remain a faithful follower. Trouble and hardship are a part of life, but I will protect you and provide for you. Adhere to your commitment to me. Trust in me. In all things, I will work for your good, because you love me. You are more than conquerors. You are a child of the King.

No power on earth or in heaven; nothing in all of creation, will separate you from my love. I love you like no other. My love for you is true. My love for you is everlasting. Nothing you do will make me love you less. Nothing you do will make me love you more. My love for you is constant and consistent. I love you no matter what. I love you in all circumstances.

I love you so much that I sent my one and only Son to die for you. He has won the war. He has conquered death and the grave. He has risen from the dead and sealed your redemption. He sits at my right hand and intercedes for you. Day and night he pleads your case before me. You are alive because the depth of my love for you is so great. My love for you never wanes, but only increases because of him. My precious child, I love you.

In the same way, the Spirit helps us in our weakness. We do not know what we ought to pray, but the Spirit himself intercedes for us with groans that words cannot express. And he who searches our hearts knows the mind of the Spirit, because the Spirit intercedes for the saints in accordance with God's will. (Romans 8:26-27)

Divine Intercession

My dear one, do you feel powerless and defenseless? Are you in a fragile, vulnerable state of mind? Has the wind been removed from your sails? Has your current trial zapped you of your energy and emotional stability? Do not fear. Do not give up hope. I am the rock you may rest upon in your times of helplessness. When your own spirit is too weak, and you don't have the words to pray, I am here. I am God's Holy Spirit within you. I will cry out to God for you in your place. God knows your heart and my mind. I will pray on your behalf in agreement with God's will.

I do not speak of my own accord. I speak only what I hear from the Father. I will remind you of your friend, Jesus, and all he has done for you. I have access to all of God's goodness, and I will make it known to you. Everything I do is done to the glory of the Father and the Son. My groans for your strength, help, and restoration, honor and please God.

Let the light of God's goodness pierce the darkness in your soul. The darkness of evil will give way to the light of truth. I will guide you to the truth, and the truth will bring you liberty. God, in his sovereignty, has the power to destroy any strongholds that bind you up. The chains that hold you captive will fall to the ground in pieces. No longer will you be vulnerable and exposed out in the open. The enemy will not have his way with you. I will gather you under my wing of protection, and strengthen you to stand your ground.

When your heart has been renewed, you will again lift your voice to the Lord. Be grateful for my intervention during your time of despair. Give thanks and praise the God who sent me to you. You are never alone. I am with you always. You have the attention of God at all times. I am your divine intercessor. All glory, honor, and praise be given to the King of the earth.

I know what it is to be in need, and I know what it is to have plenty. I have learned the secret of being content in any and every situation, whether well fed or hungry, whether living in plenty or in want. I can do everything through him who gives me strength. (Philippians 4:12-13)

Be Content

My dear sweet child, you know I am speaking to you in your heart. You have been swallowed up in worldly desires. Your heart is set on the things of the earth when it should be set on things above. Delight yourself in me, and I will put my desires in your heart. The things of this earth will be destroyed or stolen from you. Build your wealth in the riches of heaven, and live in prosperity in this life and the next. Spend time with me, and I will hide my treasure in your heart.

Discontent breeds only more unhappiness. It will rob you of all your joy. Choose to be happy in any and every situation you find yourself. Whether you have unmet needs, or you possess more than you require, be pleased in me. When your belly is full of food, or when it growls in hunger, be satisfied in me. You can face any situation, and perform any task, because I arm you with my strength. You can be impoverished or affluent, but your happiness rests with me.

Be satisfied in your current situation. A faster car does not bring permanent contentment. A bigger home will not offer you lasting joy. A better job may not be my best for you. Fame and popularity will not fill your cravings. Find your pleasure in a relationship with me. Enjoy the feast I have prepared before your very eyes. I am all that you need. I will fill every hole in your heart. Every longing you have, will be met with my presence. Appreciate the greater gifts I give you. My love, my forgiveness, my inheritance, my mercy, my peace, my wisdom, and my Spirit are all yours to enjoy. Be content in your present circumstance. I will give you the strength to do all things. Be strong in your resolve to find lasting joy in me.

Then they can train the younger women to love their husbands and children, to be self-controlled and pure, to be busy at home, to be kind, and to be subject to their husbands, so that no one will malign the word of God. Similarly, encourage the young men to be self-controlled. In everything set them an example by doing what is good. In your teaching, show integrity, seriousness and soundness of speech that cannot be condemned, so that those who oppose you may be ashamed because they have nothing bad to say about us. (Titus 2:4-8)

Teach and Do Good

I have called you to train the next generation. This will be challenging for you, as it should be. You need to be at the top of your game. As it is with children, many things are caught, not taught. To be a godly role model is of utmost importance. You must set a good example by doing what is good. Show integrity by practicing what you teach. Be serious with your instruction. Be full of wisdom, and speak reliably, with accuracy. Do not take this lightly.

To be a good role model, you must be intentional about spending time with me every day. Linger in the Scriptures daily. Be in prayer for those you influence and instruct. Seek me first in all things. Delight yourself in me, and I will give you the desires of your heart. Set goals for your time together, and keep your focus on me. Speak with me prior to each of your times together. Invite me into all your meetings. Where two or more are gathered, I will be there.

Enjoy your time with me together. Keep your instruction new and fresh. Be in tune to the leading of the Holy Spirit. Be willing to go wherever the Spirit leads you. Listen more than you talk. When you utter a word, be real and vulnerable. Speak from your heart and be transparent. Let them know that, while you don't have it all together, with my help you have made it through many tough times. Share yourself with your younger brother or sister in the faith. Share your trials and joys alike.

Lean on me, and let me be the glue that binds you together in Christ. You are not the fixer or the healer. Usher those you mentor into my presence. Bring them to me, and let me be the one who does the transformation. Help them to become more dependent on me. Show them that they can trust me for all things. Be strong and tender, firm and compassionate. Be Jesus by their side.

The best thing about this assignment is, in the process of bringing another closer to me, you will also be in my presence consistently. Remain in me always, and I will remain in you. Awesome things will be accomplished as you lead the next generation to me. Abundant blessings are yours to behold, when you remain in me, and instruct the young men and young women who will be the leaders of the future. Show them my goodness. Teach and do good things.

Create in me a pure heart, O God, and renew a steadfast spirit within me. Do not cast me from your presence or take your Holy Spirit from me. Restore to me the joy of your salvation and grant me a willing spirit, to sustain me. (Psalm 51:10-12)

Renew Your Spirit

My loyal daughter, when you place your trust in me, I will deliver you from yourself. Give me your heart, and I will wash it whiter than snow. Surrender your heart to me, and I will return your innocence to you. You will be my spotless lamb. I will remove all your iniquities. You will remain in my presence for all the days to come. I will not cast you out. I have prepared a place for you for all of eternity.

Dedicate your life to me, and I will renew your spirit. My Spirit will remain in your heart; I will not remove it from you. Commit your way to me daily, and I will make your righteousness shine like the first light of day. Submit yourself to me, and I will award you with an enthusiastic spirit to keep you going. I will replenish your joy, and deliver you from your selfishness. You cannot escape me. My eyes are on you at all times. You cannot hide yourself from me. I know where you are, because I am there also.

Has your happiness been removed from you? Delight in me, and I will be your newfound joy. My Spirit within you is your life force. Your spirit will be restored by mine. I will reignite the flame of passion within you. You have a new reason to live—it is I. I am your lifeblood—the only thing that keeps you going. I have brought about your existence, and I will sustain you.

I cherish each moment you spend with me. Your heart belongs to me, and I am pleased. Remain faithful in your walk with me. I will not dismiss your requests. I will give you an unwavering spirit. Stand firm in the path I set your feet on. Persevere down the road I lay before you. Your heart is right with me. I will honor your request and renew your spirit.

Then Jesus told his disciples a parable to show them that they should always pray and not give up . . . And the Lord said, "Listen to what the unjust judge says. And will not God bring about justice for his chosen ones, who cry out to him day and night? Will he keep putting them off? I tell you, he will see that they get justice, and quickly. However, when the Son of Man comes, will he find faith on the earth?" (Luke 18:1, 6-8)

Pray and Don't Give Up

My child, you must be persistent in prayer. Pray continually, day and night. Pray faithfully in the Spirit at all times. I never grow tired of hearing your prayers—even the same prayers time and again. When you pray earnestly, with sincerity, I know that you are passionate about the subject of your prayer. Your passion ignites a fire within me. When you eagerly lay your requests before me, I listen attentively. You are my chosen one, and I will deal with you honestly and fairly. I will not delay in accomplishing your desires.

When you pray to me, I am near you. I hear the prayers of the righteous and accept them. When you call on me, I do not reject your requests. You will receive whatever you ask for in my name. Keep asking. Plead your case before me. I urge you to place your petitions at my feet. Devote yourself to prayer when you are alone and when you are in community. There is never a wrong time to pray. I hear you whether you utter one word or a thousand words. When you cannot pray out loud to me, present your silent requests to me. I know your thoughts, and when you do not know what to pray, my Spirit will pray on your behalf.

Persevere in faithfulness, and you will receive what God has promised. Do not shrink back in your faith when your prayers are not answered in your timing. My timing is perfect. My righteous ones live by faith, because they believe, and they are saved. Be sure of what you anticipate, and certain in the God you do not see. Believe he exists, and earnestly seek him. Great is the reward of the faithful. The time is coming when I will return without delay. When I come again, will I find you faithful?

Let the word of Christ dwell in you richly as you teach and admonish one another with all wisdom, and as you sing psalms, hymns, and spiritual songs with gratitude in your hearts to God. And whatever you do, whether in word or deed, do it all in the name of the Lord Jesus, giving thanks to God the Father through him. (Colossians 3:16-17)

Let the Word Dwell in You

I am the Word, and I give you my Word. Let my Word dwell in you abundantly. To accomplish this, you must be in the Scripture daily reading my Word, so that you may call on it when you need it the most. You must be filled with the Spirit. Let the spirit of peace rule in your heart. I am calling you to peace. My Spirit lives in your heart and brings my peace to your soul. Be submissive to the Holy Spirit whom I have sent to dwell in you. He will also remind you of my words and my deeds, so that you may live your life like mine.

Before you may reprove another, you must first remove the obstruction from your own eye. See clearly the offenses that separate you from me. Confess your own sin, before you call out the sin of another. Then, rely on the wisdom of my Word, to teach others my truth. Do not be condescending with your words. Do not insult or wound the one you admonish. Be gentle and loving as you speak my words of wisdom to your brother or sister in Christ. Correct each other in humility because you are not above reproach. As I have dealt with you, so you must be gracious and merciful in your rebuke.

Be thankful in all circumstances. With a grateful heart, let my Word dwell in you richly as you sing your songs and hymns to God. Give thanks to God, through my name in God's honor, so that the Father and I will be glorified. Whatever you do, do it with your whole heart. It is I, the Lord Christ, you are serving. I will reward you with justice. Take your gift of inheritance from me. I am the Word. I am the Prince of Peace. Let my Word dwell in you, and my peace rule your heart. Remain in my Word, and my Word will remain in you.

Chapter 8

PROCLAIM ME

When we remain in him,
and his words remain in us,
we will be fruitful.

To the Jews who had believed him, Jesus said, "If you hold to my teaching, you are really my disciples. Then you will know the truth, and the truth will set you free." (John 8:31-32)

The Truth

I am a jealous God, a God of vengeance. I am in control. Do not turn from me, but do my will. Do not act as if you do not know me. I am God. I have set you apart. I have separated the sheep from the goats. You are my sheep. I call you by name. You have received the gift of eternal life. It is now your job to preach the truth to those who do not yet know. I have shown you the truth. I am the truth.

You know the way. Walk in the way, and do not depart from it. Lead others to the way. I am the way. So many people do not know the way to me—but you do. You must teach them, show them. They have heard the name Jesus, yet they do not know the man. How will you accomplish this? Where do you begin? Begin in your own home first. Then, work on your street. Next, visit the suburbs. Like a ripple in the water, so my truth will spread to the vast seas. You are a drop in the water. You are a mere mortal, but my power is in you. Live by my Spirit; walk in my truth and receive my power from on high.

I will empower you to be a witness to my people. My name will be great again in the land. Wisdom I will give you. Knowledge will follow. I have made you a bright light. Let your light shine before men. Do not hide your light. There is no shadow in turning to me. You cannot hide in the secret place. On that, I will lock the doors. You must gather up your things, and camp out in the open fields. Pull up your tent stakes, and present yourself to the masses. I go with you. I do not send you alone. You are my spokesperson. I will speak through you. I will give you my words. You are my vessel of truth.

I am your God. You are my child. I do not give you a spirit of timidity, but I will drive out all your fears. My love is perfect. To you, I give my righteousness. Like the dawn of a new day, you are clothed in my splendor. You were created with one purpose in mind: you will bear witness to the truth. I am the truth, and the truth will set you free.

Do not worry or be anxious about this news. I will prepare the way for you. I will equip you and arm you for this battle. I will protect you from the wolves. I will hold back your enemies. You may suffer in my name, but my reward is great. Lend your ear to my teachings. I am the Lord. I am the God of truth. I am the Creator of all the earth. I will bring my people back home to me. They will know the truth, and the truth will set them free as well.

You are a messenger—a messenger of the truth. Do not give in to your own ways, but seek me in everything you do. I will direct your paths. I will clear the road ahead of you. Pay attention to my voice. Listen with a clear mind. Follow my instructions, honor me, and your life will be long and prosperous. These are my plans. Prepare yourself for the journey ahead. Remain in me. Proclaim me.

They replied, "Believe in the Lord Jesus, and you will be saved—you and your household." . . . and the whole family was filled with joy, because they had come to believe in God. (Acts 16:31,34b)

A Family Filled with Joy

So you believe in me. You experience the joy of a life in Christ. Your salvation is secure because you have given your life to me. You have confessed your sins and asked me to be your Savior and Lord. We experience an intimate bond. Life is good.

What about your own household? What about your extended family? Do they believe in me? Do they see me in your life? Does your face reflect me? Is your joy apparent? Do they feel my love through you? Do you proclaim me in your home? Are you Jesus to your family?

My beloved, I have showered you with my love. I have given you good gifts. You are living a full life. Trials will come, but I walk with you through your trials. Hardships are inevitable, but I will provide for you. The joy in your heart does not have to fade because you walk through fire. You do not walk alone.

When will you be my witness to your closest family and friends? What will it take to light a fire in your heart for the lost? You have a daily influence on people who do not know me yet. Will their eternal destiny be a result of your silence or your testimony?

The joy in your heart is a direct result of a life in me. The peace in your life is not of your own making. The fact that you are loved by the King of the universe is not something to take for granted. How awesome it would be if your home was filled with a family of believers. How comforting it would be to know that your friends will spend eternity in my presence. It is not enough to believe and be complacent. The ones you love may not understand. They may not know there is a more excellent way. They may not have heard the good news yet. Will you be the one to tell them? Will your family be filled with joy because they believe in God?

Come and listen, all you who fear God; let me tell you what he has done for me. I cried out to him with my mouth; his praise was on my tongue. If I had cherished sin in my heart, the Lord would not have listened; but God has surely listened and heard my voice in prayer. Praise be to God, who has not rejected my prayer or withheld his love from me! (Psalm 66:16-20)

I Listen to You

My child, I do not desire any separation from you. I hear your cries of repentance. I forgive you of your sins. I will not withhold my love from you. I hear your voice in prayer today. I will not reject your pleas for help. I listen intently to all you say to me. I enjoy the praises and adoration you lift up to me. I appreciate the confession on your lips. I recognize your thankfulness for all I do. I know your needs and hear your requests. I answer your prayers. I know what is best for you.

Share with others what I have done for you. Boldly shout it from the mountaintops. Proclaim my goodness to all who hear your voice. Let my ways be made known to those who remain in darkness. I want no separation from any of my creation. I aspire to be reconciled to all people on the earth. I want to change the heart of the unrepentant person. Teach them my ways. Tell of my wonderful acts. Let them know their sin offends me. Open their eyes to the truth of my salvation. My grace and mercy are available to all who call on me in repentance.

My child, I love you with all I have. I listen to your voice and hear your prayers. I love it when you call on me. I delight in the time you devote to me. You are my precious creation. I designed you with my purposes in mind. Bring me with you wherever you go. Call on me any time of the day or night. I am always with you, even when you do not feel my presence. Invite me into your daily walk. I will not refuse you. Share me with a friend or a stranger. Make known my ways, and the things I have done for you. Delight yourself in me, and be my shining light for all to see.

In that day you will say: "Give thanks to the Lord, call on his name; make known among the nations what he has done, and proclaim that his name is exalted. Sing to the Lord, for he has done glorious things; let this be known to all the world. Shout aloud and sing for joy, people of Zion, for great is the Holy One of Israel among you." (Isaiah 12:4-6)

Let All the World Know

Give thanks! You are my child. Do not be afraid to announce to the world that you belong to me. Proclaim that I am the Most High God, and yet I am your friend. Exalt my name over all the earth. Make known to the world my mighty acts. Sing your praises; I have done great things for you. Shout aloud; the Holy One is with you—not just with you, but within you. You have direct access to the great and glorious King of kings—the God of the universe—on a daily basis, minute by minute.

I AM. I am the God of your salvation. I saved you from a life of sin and death. I sacrificed my Son in your place. I paid the ransom for your soul. I closed the gap of sin that separated us. I brought you into my presence, and clothed you with my righteousness. You have the promise of living with me in eternity. Now this is something to get excited about! Share me with all you meet. Do not be bashful or afraid. I will give you the confidence of a mighty warrior—one who has been skillfully trained for battle. March into the wind, I am by your side. Raise your sword and declare my sovereignty saying, "My God reigns!"

I am majestic and powerful. Do not try to hide me under a rock. If you do not boast on my name, the very rocks will cry out. Sing to me a new song—a song that glorifies my name. Worship me with adoration. Lift your praises to the skies. Tell of the wonderful things I have done. I have pulled you up out of the pit. I delivered you from a life of slavery, and brought you into a land of plenty. I redeemed you. My name is worthy to be praised.

Lay claim to the abundant life in me. Devote yourself to prayer. Spend time in my Word. Spend time with me. This is worship as much as lifting your voice in song. Do not let the fire I set within you die down to a mere ember. Fan the flames of your passion for me. Dedicate

172

your life to serving me with gladness. Pay tribute to me, and tell of my works with songs of joy. Give thanks for my unfailing love. Be my witness, and share my love with those who have lost their way. Show them the way to a new life in Christ. I am worthy, and worthy of your praise. Do not turn down your bed at night without giving me thanks. Extol your Savior, God, and King!

"But you will receive power when the Holy Spirit comes on you; and you will be my witnesses in Jerusalem, and in all Judea and Samaria, and to the ends of the earth." (Acts 1:8)

My Witnesses

My dear children, you are my priceless treasures. You have experienced my sacrificial and unconditional love for you. You know the truth of my saving grace, but some do not. Salvation is found in no one else, yet many people still put their trust in false gods, and worship idols. You have received my peace and have first-hand knowledge of my mercy; but others live at war within their souls, and do not have the assurance of my forgiveness. You know my voice, and you hear my will, but communities near you and citizens of foreign nations have never even heard my name.

The harvest is ripe for the picking, but few will gather it in for me. Will you reap the crops from the soil I have watered and fertilized myself? What I ask of you is nothing more than proclaiming my goodness to the ears that have not yet heard. You have personally experienced a life in me. You know where you came from, and where you are going. You received my forgiveness, and you hold onto the promise of spending an eternity with me.

I do not send you out on your own. My Holy Spirit lives within you. Utilize the power of the Spirit I sent you. You do not have to travel to Africa to be my witness. Start with your neighbor, your co-worker, or friend. The more they know you and trust you, the better the chance of conversion. It is my desire that all peoples of the earth know me, and confess me as their Lord. I have called you to be the farmer of my fields. Whether you till the soil, sow the seed, plant the vine, or water the crop, you will be doing my will. Will you be my witnesses, and testify to the truth of my goodness and my salvation? Proclaim me wherever you are. Make known my name among all people, and the yield of the harvest will expand exponentially.

How beautiful on the mountains are the feet of those who bring good news, who proclaim peace, who bring good tidings, who proclaim salvation, who say to Zion, "Your God reigns!" (Isaiah 52:7)

Your God Reigns!

My dear one, will you proclaim my goodness? I have set your feet upon the mountains so that your voice would be heard over all the earth. You have good news to share. I am that good news. Do not be shy. Do not be afraid. Do not hold your tongue in this moment. This is the time to celebrate. This is the time to rejoice. Your God reigns!

I have brought you out of the captivity of your sin, and given you a life of freedom. I gave the life of my Son who suffered in your place. Your sin was punished, and you were redeemed through the obedient act of sacrifice that my Son willingly made for you. You are no longer separated from me by your sin. Your sins are forgiven; you have been washed clean in the blood of the Lamb. You were saved by my good work in Christ, not by any good works of your own. My grace alone has provided the way for you to have everlasting life. Do not be afraid to proclaim this great news. Proclaim it from the mountaintops, so that all of the world may hear and know, "Your God reigns!"

I have delivered you from all your despair, and given you a life of peace. Your hopelessness has been replaced with a newfound hope in me. I am the reason you live the abundant life. I am the anchor for your soul. I comfort you in your distress. I protect you from your enemy. I provide the nourishment for your spirit. I am the object of your faith. Is any of this enough to make you want to shout, "Thank you, Jesus?" Do not let your hands hang limp. Lift them up in praise of my holy name. Proclaim me from the mountaintops. Make your voice heard from the valleys. Wherever your feet take you in life, declare my goodness and mercy. I am the God who saves. I have saved you and made you whole. Share my love with the world. Bring my good news, and proclaim my peace. Your God reigns!

Let the peace of Christ rule in your hearts, since as members of one body you were called to peace. And be thankful. (Colossians 3:15)

Called to Peace

My beloved child, you are mine, and you have been called to peace. Let my peace control your heart. There is no reason to worry. There is nothing you shall fear. You have the peace of knowing that I am with you. I will protect you from all harm. I will lead you with my wisdom. I will direct your paths. I am in control of all things. You may cast your cares upon me. I give you a peace beyond your comprehension. The world does not give you the peace I give. I have given you my Spirit—the Spirit is life and peace. Be thankful for this gift.

Set my words deep within your heart. Spend time in the Scripture day and night. Bathe yourself in my words. Saturate yourself with the Word. I am the Word, and my Spirit lives in you. The Spirit will remind you of what I have said. Let my words dwell in you abundantly. Before you can teach or reprove another, you must gain all wisdom from my Word. Do not rebuke another of your own accord, but according to my Word only. The Spirit will guide you in all truth. Speak the truth in love.

Give thanks in all things. Sing to me a new song with gratitude in your heart. Whatever you do, do it in my name, showing your appreciation to God through me. Let your lips sing in admiration of me, and tell of my wonderful acts. I have come to give you a new life. Share my goodness with all you meet. Be grateful for God's plan of salvation, which renews your life in Christ. Do not keep silent. Share the grace of God with all you know, and I will add to God's kingdom here on earth and in heaven.

Great is the Lord and most worthy of praise; his greatness no one can fathom. One generation will commend your works to another; they will tell of your mighty acts. They will speak of the glorious splendor of your majesty, and I will meditate on your wonderful works. They will tell of the power of your awesome works, and I will proclaim your great deeds. (Psalm 145:3-6)

The Next Generation

My blessed child, will you proclaim me to the next generation? Commend my works to your children. Tell of my mighty acts. Rejoice in my glorious splendor. Meditate on my wonderful works. Tell of my awesome power. Proclaim my great deeds. Your children will know and experience me through you. Let my name be praised in your own household.

You have the most influence on the ones who come after you. Pass along my goodness to those who will receive your inheritance. The riches of the treasure you lay up for yourself in heaven must be passed down to your children, and your children's children. The testimony of your eternal wealth in me is the greatest witness you have to give. It is the greatest gift of all. Proclaim my grace and my salvation to all those who will listen. It is the most precious legacy you will leave behind for them.

I have done great things for you. Do not let your mouth be silent. Do not let your hands hang down by your side. Shout with glory to all the earth. Lift your hands in praise of my name. Declare my goodness to all those who can hear you. Tell of the greatness of my love. Share my excellent works with your guests. Announce my mighty deeds to those who gather around your table. Communicate what I have done for you. Tell of my magnificent greatness. Impart the light of my truth and dispel all darkness. The ears of your audience are attentive to your voice. Will you proclaim me to the next generation?

"The good man brings good things out of the good stored up in his heart, and the evil man brings evil things out of the evil stored up in his heart. For out of the overflow of his heart his mouth speaks." (Luke 6:45)

Speak From Your Heart

My beloved one, the only way to be sure your speech is pleasing to God is to yield your heart to him. If your heart is full of hatred and disdain, the words that roll off your tongue will not gain God's approval. Whatever fills up your heart will spill over into your mouth. Discipline your tongue, and exercise self-control with your speech. Get your heart right before you say one word. If your emotions are in a volatile state, hold your tongue, or you will surely regret what you say.

Be diligent about accumulating only good things in your heart. Do not let evil rule your heart. If you love God, the love of God is in your heart. You will speak the truth of God's love. When you ask God for a wise and discerning heart, words of wisdom will flow from your lips. If you walk in integrity of heart, no lies will proceed from your mouth; but if your heart has been hardened, your words will seem cruel and harsh. Strive to obtain a positive outlook, and your language will build another up; but focus on the negative, and your tongue will boast judgment and condemnation.

When you delight yourself in me, I will fill your heart with my goodness. Out of your mouth will flow the goodness of your heart; but walk in the ways of the wicked, and store evil in your heart, and you will spew malicious deceptions with your tongue. Guard your heart from the attacks of your enemy, and get rid of all iniquity. Fill your heart with my precepts, and obey my commands. A joyful tongue reflects a heart full of joy. The heart of the wise will guide the tongue to articulate wisdom. Be fluent in the language of God. Set your heart on the things above. Fill your heart with God's goodness, and then speak from your heart.

Then Jesus came to them and said, "All authority in heaven and on earth has been given to me. Therefore go and make disciples of all nations, baptizing them in the name of the Father and of the Son and of the Holy Spirit, and teaching them to obey everything I have commanded you. And surely I will be with you always, to the very end of the age." (Matthew 28:18-20)

Make Disciples of All Nations

You are my disciples when you obey my commands. You are my followers when you live by the laws I lay down. When you believe in me, I give you great responsibilities. Live a life that is pleasing to me. You need not be concerned about anything else, but listen to my voice only, and follow my instructions. I have laid out a good path for you to follow. Adhere to my teachings, and let your actions represent me. I am the object of your faith. I give meaning and purpose to your life. Let my light shine from your hearts. Let my goodness flow through your veins. Let my love and good graces overflow from your lips.

Do not keep my love to yourself. Love others with the love you have been afforded. Do not hold your tongue in silence, but proclaim my salvation to everyone you meet. Teach them to listen to me, and obey my instructions as you, yourself, are doing. Gather support in my name. I will be with you at all times. I do not send you out on your own. I go with you. Each step you take is guided by me. I have cleared the road you walk down. I remove the obstacles that are set in front of you. Nothing will keep you from proclaiming my grace. No barriers will hinder the mission I give you. No destructive efforts of the evil one will prevail.

You will plant good seeds in the fertile soil I provide for you. I prepare the ground for the sowing. Do not waste my seed in the sandy areas; the roots will have nothing to cling to. I give you the fields that are ready for harvest. They are ripe for the picking. Waste no time on the crop that has been choked out by weeds. Your labor will be in vain. Go where I send you, and concentrate on the task I set before you. Be prepared to share the reason for your hope. Be gentle and loving in every word and deed. I am with you always, now and forever more.

"He who listens to you listens to me; he who rejects you rejects me; but he who rejects me rejects him who sent me." (Luke 10:16)

They Will Listen to You

Blessed are the meek, for they shall inherit the earth. Blessed are you in your gentleness. You will win many souls in my kingdom here on the earth. In your humbleness and obedience to me, you bring me all the glory. You understand that your great debt was paid by me. You willingly submit yourself to me because of what I have accomplished for you. The world knows who you once were, and now they see what you have become. You are a key player in the advancement of my kingdom, both here on earth and in heaven.

Do not keep this great mystery to yourself. There is a reason for the transformation that has taken place in you. I am the reason for your hope. Will you be my witness? Will you testify to the greatness of my love for all mankind? Will you share my plan of salvation? They will listen to you because you are not arrogant. You are humble in heart and gracious in deeds. Your gentle spirit appeals to those who surround you. There is something different in your talk and in your walk. When you speak, they will listen. If they listen to you, they will listen to me. If they accept you, they will accept me.

Those who refuse you, will refuse me. Those who reject me, reject my Father also. I and my Father are one. If they do not believe in me, they do not believe in the Father. They are not my sheep. My sheep know my voice and listen to me. I know my sheep, and my sheep follow me. Those who reject me and my Father will surely perish; but I give the gift of eternal life to those who accept me as their Savior, and accept what I have done for them. My Father has given them to me. What my Father has given me is greater than all. No one can take that away from me. No one can snatch them away from the Father. I am in my Father, and my Father is in me. Those who accept me, belong to me and to my Father.

Sing to the Lord a new song; sing to the Lord, all the earth. Sing to the Lord, praise his name; proclaim his salvation day after day. Declare his glory among the nations, his marvelous deeds among all peoples. For great is the Lord and most worthy of praise; he is to be feared above all gods. (Psalm 96:1-4)

Proclaim My Salvation

Let heaven and earth sing a new song. Each day a fresh melody they sing. All the peoples of the earth will rejoice in my name. My awesome deeds shall be declared by all men. Kings will bow down before me. All authority in heaven and earth belongs to me. My name shall be worshipped above all other names. Praise songs will ring out in harmony from every tongue. I am great and worthy of your admiration.

Look to me all ye peoples of the earth. Hold me up above all other gods. I have rescued you from the hands of your opponent. I have delivered you from your iniquities. I have removed your punishment from you. My love for you is perfect and unending. I have adopted you as my children. I even call you my friends. Declare my glorious works. Proclaim my righteousness among all nations of the world. My actions will speak for themselves.

The rocks will not remain silent. They lift their voices in honor and praise of my holy name. Mountains will crumble in humbleness before me. The heavens will rain down my righteousness and the seas will roll back from the shores. Everything on the earth is under my command. In the greatness of my awesome power, I reign over every living thing. I am excellent and most worthy of your praise. Tell of my generous act of salvation. Share the gift of my grace every day. Boast of my compassions and mercies. They never fail; they are new every morning. My loving kindness and forgiveness offer blessings to all of humanity.

In glory and power I will return to you again. My salvation belongs to all who believe in my name. Confess me with your mouth. You will have nothing to fear. Death will not hold you in the grave. I will raise you up, and you will spend eternity in the heavens with me.

*My tongue will speak of your righteousness and of your praises all day long.
(Psalm 35:28)*

Speak of My Righteousness

Blessed are those who acclaim me, who sing of my praises from the break of dawn until the sun goes down. Blessed are those who tell of my wonderful acts. Make known among the nations the awesome deeds I have done. Let all the peoples of the earth fear the name of the Lord. Let the kings of the earth revere my glory. I am the Alpha and the Omega, the Beginning and the End. I existed before the beginning of time, and I will remain long after its end.

I created the earth with its splendor; the heavens I formed with my own hands. All the peoples of the earth will proclaim my righteousness. My name will be declared in all corners of the world. My honesty and integrity do not fail. My justice remains forever. My throne has been established through righteousness. My honor will last for all times. I clothe my children in robes of righteousness, and cause their faces to shine like the sun. My glory is reflected in all who seek me and understand my greatness.

Commend my works to all generations. Tell of the riches of my splendor. Admire me in the worship sanctuary. Sing praises to me in the courts of justice. Honor me in the presence of your enemies. Lift up your hands in celebration of my works. I have done great things for you. Praise my name with hearts of gratitude. Proclaim my salvation day after day. I have plucked you from the pit of eternal destruction. I will deliver you from the grave.

Extol me with all of your heart. My saints will exalt my name. Honor me with the words of your lips. Adore me with music and song. Give thanks to me because of my goodness, and forever give praise to my holy name. I have given you victory through my Son, Jesus Christ, the Lord. I am your Savior, God and King. Sing your praise to me all day long.

Devote yourselves to prayer, being watchful and thankful. And pray for us, too, that God may open a door for our message, so that we may proclaim the mystery of Christ, for which I am in chains. Pray that I may proclaim it clearly, as I should. Be wise in the way you act toward outsiders; make the most of every opportunity. Let your conversation be always full of grace, seasoned with salt, so that you may know how to answer everyone. (Colossians 4:2-6)

Make the Most of Every Opportunity

My friend, do you make the most of every opportunity to share the message of my saving grace? So many times I open a door for you, and you do not walk through it. You ask for chances to share your testimony, and when I afford you the chance, you don't see it. When you ask me for anything in my name, consider it done. The first thing you should do is ask. Pray and then be watchful for the opening. Do not be anxious, but be thankful for the entrance I have opened. I have provided you with the way to proclaim the mystery of Christ.

Be devoted to prayer when it comes to being my witness. Pray that you will proclaim clearly the message of truth. I have seasoned you with the salt of my truth. You are living proof of my saving grace. You are the salt of the earth. Season those around you with the same salt. You are the light of the world. Do not hide yourself, but shine brightly for all to see. Give light to everyone around you so that your Father in heaven may be praised.

Always be ready to answer everyone regarding your hope. Choose words that are full of grace. Be gentle and respectful. Do not condemn or express your disapproval, but give the hope of eternity to the one stuck in mortality. Entrust the mystery of Christ to the ears that are ready to listen, and the heart that is ready to grasp it. If the door is open, I have prepared the way for you. Do not be silent about the hope I have given you when you are asked. Express the reason for your unending joy. I give you the keys to heaven. Are you willing to open the door for someone else? You are my kingdom connection. The ones you connect with will receive me and the guarantee of my promises. Don't miss an opportunity to build my kingdom.

But in your hearts set apart Christ as Lord. Always be prepared to give an answer to everyone who asks you to give the reason for the hope that you have. But do this with gentleness and respect, keeping a clear conscience, so that those who speak maliciously against your good behavior in Christ may be ashamed of their slander. (1 Peter 3:15-16)

The Reason for Your Hope

My child of promise, I am the reason for your hope. I gave you the hope and the assurance of life everlasting. I gave my life for you so that you could live both now and forever. Live in the hope of spending an eternity with me in heaven. You are living a life of promise in my kingdom here on earth. You are being transformed in front of an audience. You have discarded your old ways of doing things. You are living in the newness of Christ. You have caught the attention of the world. Now what will you do on the stage?

I am asking you to be prepared. Do not forsake the dress rehearsal. Practice your lines so that when you are asked, you will have the right answer. Always be ready to communicate the reason for the hope that you have. I am your hope. Share the gift of my hope with the one who eagerly seeks an answer from you. Your good behavior has caught the attention of the one who knew you before. You are a changed individual. Hope is written all over your face. Hope springs through every decision you make. Your expectations now exceed the dreams you once had. You look forward to what lies ahead of you.

In your answer, set me apart as your Lord. Always be gentle and respectful of the one with whom you speak. Do not condemn or be condescending in your reply. Simply share who I am with your inquisitive friend. Reveal what I mean to you, and what I have done for you. Be vulnerable and transparent in your conversation. Give them no reason to slander you, but win them over with your chaste and respectful behavior. Remember, I am with you. This opportunity to testify about me is one of the steps in your journey of transformation. Do not be fearful. My perfect love casts out all your fears. I love you perfectly. Share my love.

The heavens declare the glory of God; the skies proclaim the work of his hands. Day after day they pour forth speech; night after night they display knowledge. There is no speech or language where their voice is not heard. Their voice goes out into all the earth, their words to the ends of the world. (Psalm 19:1-4)

The Skies Proclaim My Work

My precious daughter, I ask you to proclaim me. By word or deed, declare my glory. Make known your God among the nations. Even the heavens affirm my brilliance. Even the skies proclaim my wonderful works. Every day they speak of my goodness. Every night they demonstrate understanding of me. The sun rises and sets at the sound of my voice. The moon regulates the tide at my instruction. The stars were hung in the heavens by me. The beautiful rainbow forms after the storm. Everything puts forth an effort according to my purpose. There is no continent where their voice is not heard. The skies proclaim me day and night to the very ends of the earth.

You were formed in your mother's womb by my instruction. I created the color of your hair and numbered each one. I breathed the breath of life into your tiny lungs. Your heart started its rhythm at the sound of my voice. Your name is written on my palms. I designed each day of your life before one of them came to be. You were made in my image. You are good. To know and understand the inner workings of a human being speaks volumes of my spectacular masterpiece. Your form alone demonstrates my magnificent splendor. You are the crown of my creation.

Be like the heavens, and declare my glory. Imitate the skies, and proclaim my great works. Use your voice to proclaim my good deeds. Let the whole earth see me written on your face. Shine brightly in this dark world. Hold my light out for all to see and touch. Tell all peoples about my perfect love. Speak about my righteousness. Convey my awesome plan of salvation. Walk the path that I have walked. Follow in my footsteps. Be Jesus to the world.

Be imitators of God, therefore, as dearly loved children and live a life of love, just as Christ loved us and gave himself up for us as a fragrant offering and sacrifice to God. (Ephesians 5:1)

Live a Life of Love

My blessed children, you are children of light. You no longer live in darkness. You know the truth of Jesus. Your minds have been renewed in the ways of Christ. Do not return to your former ways. Be made new in the attitude of your minds. You were created to be like God. You were set apart in holiness and righteousness, as dearly loved children of the Father. Live your lives as Christ lived. Live a life of love. Submit yourself to God, and demonstrate his love to the world. Let your actions speak louder than your words.

Put away your former ways and the beliefs you once held onto. Let your spirit be renewed by my Spirit. Speak only words of truth. Let there be no falsehood in you. Do not sin because of your anger. Do not give your enemy access to you. Find your reward in the work of your hands, and share what you have with the poor. Let your speech be wholesome, always encouraging others. Do not hold onto bitterness, but forgive one another, as you have been forgiven. Be full of compassion and generous with kindness.

In this way, by living a life of love, you will be my witness. Proclaim me in the way you live; speak of me by the loving things you do. Do not be selfish, but always treat each other as better than yourselves. Put another's interests ahead of your own. Be willing to lay down your life for a friend. Pray for your enemies. Do not entertain greed or impure thoughts. Do not practice sexual immorality. Always be thankful for all that you have.

Live in the light of God's truth. The fruit of God's light is goodness, righteousness, and truth. Remain in God, and the righteousness of God will remain in you. By living a life of love, you express God's truth and his righteousness. The testimony of your life will produce the fruit of God's goodness and light. Be fruitful and multiply followers of the light.

It is written: "I believed; therefore I have spoken." With that same spirit of faith we also believe and therefore speak, because we know that the one who raised the Lord Jesus from the dead will also raise us with Jesus and present us with you in his presence. (2 Corinthians 4:13-14)

Believe and Speak

My dear one, do you believe? If you believe, you should also speak. The faith that allows you to believe, in turn, permits you to speak. You have the faith in knowing Jesus Christ saved you from your sin. You believe in your heart that I raised Jesus from the dead. You are confident that I will raise you also when the time comes. You rely on my gift of grace as the plan of your salvation. You put all your hope and trust in me.

Will you remain silent? You believe and you are saved, but your friend is not. You have the assurance of spending an eternity with me, and your unbelieving friend has the assurance of living forever apart from me. Do you love that friend enough to speak about what you believe? Shouldn't your friend be given the same opportunity you were given? Do not leave this work to someone else or some other day. There is no one else and the time is now. Some other day may never come. Life is precious and uncertain. Speak now and offer the same gift of my grace that you yourself have received. Their eternal destination is at stake.

Profess your faith in the living God. When you actively share your faith in me, you yourself stand to gain a more complete understanding of all the fullness of Christ. By expressing the goodness of my grace and my eternal promises, you realize the awesome gift you have been given. Faith without expression is empty. Fill your heart with joy as you communicate the reason for your hope to the one who is lost in ignorance. Plant the seed, and I will water it. Your role is not to convince. Simply share what you know of me. Tell what I have done for you. Let your life reveal my truth. Let them taste and see my goodness. Speak what you believe, and you will believe, more completely, what you speak.

Day after day, in the temple courts and from house to house, they never stopped teaching and proclaiming the good news that Jesus is the Christ. (Acts 5:42)

Proclaim the Good News

My dearest child, do not hold out on me. You know the good news. You know that my Son, Jesus, is the promised Messiah. You must proclaim the good news at all times. Never stop proclaiming the good news. Day after day, wherever you find yourself, instruct others in the message of the gospel. Whether you are a teacher, a businessman, a stay-at-home mom, a pastor, a sanitation engineer, or a nurse, you can proclaim the good news every day of your life. You do not need to be gifted with speech to share what you know. Rely on me, and I will give you the words that you seek. I will prepare the hearts you touch to receive the good news.

My awesome works and generous grace are worthy of your time and efforts. You have been given the gift of life, even life eternal. Is that something that should be kept quiet? Never in any circumstance should you be afraid or ashamed to share the gift of grace that you, yourself, have received. Jesus pled for your life. I took mercy on you, and now you belong to me. You will spend eternity with me in a much better place. Will you put yourself out to plead for the life of another? Will you expose yourself and be vulnerable for the sake of another soul? Will you share the greatest gift you have ever received?

You stand forgiven. My Son's death paid the penalty for your sin. That same forgiveness is available to all who ask, but some people do not know of my grace. Some have never heard the good news. Someone took the risk of sharing the message with you. Your life changed for all of eternity. Shouldn't that opportunity be afforded to every person on this earth? Shouldn't all my creation have the chance to experience my redeeming work? Please do not keep silent when it comes to me. Express my redeeming grace to all you know. My joy is made complete in the process. That joy will spill out into your own life as well.

"He commanded us to preach to the people and to testify that he is the one whom God appointed as judge of the living and the dead. All the prophets testify about him that everyone who believes in him receives forgiveness of sins through his name." While Peter was still speaking these words, the Holy Spirit came on all who heard the message. (Acts 10:42-44)

Preach to the People

You will be my witnesses. This is what I command of you. You have faith in what you do not see. You believe in my Holy Scripture—the inerrant Word of God. You believe the testimonies that have been passed down from one generation to the next. From the first disciples that walked the earth with Jesus, to the ones who follow him today, the message of the gospel has been proclaimed throughout all generations— every nation, tribe, and tongue.

It will not stop here with you. You do not need a pulpit to preach from. You do not have to prepare a sermon or lecture, but speak from your heart. Gently teach what you know. Share my redeeming work in your life. Do not condemn another in the process. Look at where you came from. I did not condemn you. Neither should you put down your brother or your friend, instead lift him up before me. Place him at the foot of the cross. Open his eyes to my forgiving grace. Pray for his discovery of a new life in Christ.

Before you open your mouth to utter a word about me, seek me first. Listen for my voice in your thoughts, and speak the words I give you for the exact situation you are in. Each of my children must hear about me in a way that is appealing to them. I will give you the gift of knowledge when it comes to witnessing effectively to your present audience. You cannot use the same message for all people. Each person is so different and unique, his or her understanding of the gospel depends on my work in their hearts. You do not go it alone. I am by your side as you testify to my goodness. I will give you what you need to accomplish what I ask of you. As you speak, the Holy Spirit will come on all who hear your voice. Everyone who believes will receive my forgiveness. Exercise faith in me. Continue to preach to the people.

Chapter 9

GLORIFY ME

We lift up our praises to glorify God.

Note: *The first two devotionals in the "Glorify Me" chapter are written in the voice of God, while the remaining devotionals in the chapter are written in the voice of the author/reader, in order to give God the honor and glory that he desires and deserves.*

So whether you eat or drink or whatever you do, do it all for the glory of God.
(1 Corinthians 10:31)

Glorify Me

My dear child, do not be concerned about what you will eat or drink. It does not matter to me what you consume. What matters to me most is that everything you do brings glory to my name. Do not seek your own good, but the good of others, as Christ Jesus did. Love me with everything you have, and love your neighbor. Love trumps all.

Be careful what you say. The words that flow from your mouth should honor me at all times. Your words should not condemn your brother, but lift him up. Be an encouragement to all who know you. Your actions speak louder than your words, so honor me in all you do. Be kind, compassionate, loving, and merciful. Extend these qualities to those who surround you. I know you are not perfect. Rely on me. I will give you the strength and ability to model my character to people you influence.

To rely on me fully, you will need to stay close to me. Do not attempt to go through your day without me. When your eyes open in the morning, let my praises be on your lips. Before you step out of bed, be certain to connect with me. Give me a few minutes of your day before you set foot outside your home. Listen to my voice. Hear what I have to say. I know what is best for you. I have planned the same.

What you receive from me, pass along to others. Kind words, a respectful manner, a patient and tolerant character will bring you much honor in the world. Follow the example of my Son, Jesus Christ. I and my Son are one. Be like Christ to the world, so that they may know me also. Do not be concerned about winning friends for yourself, but win friends for me. Let the light of my glory shine from your face. Glorify me in all you do and say.

"Blessed are those who hunger and thirst for righteousness, for they will be filled . . . Blessed are the pure in heart, for they will see God . . . Blessed are those who are persecuted because of righteousness, for theirs is the kingdom of heaven." (Matthew 5:6, 8, 10)

Great is Your Reward

Blessed are you, my children, when you desire honesty and goodness. Blessed are you when you aspire to integrity and godliness. I will satisfy your longings. When you walk in an upright manner and pursue honor and decency, virtue will be added to your character. You have been cleansed by me. Live your life in a blameless manner. Do not submit to guilt and shame. I do not condemn you, but ask you to turn from your sinful ways, and live a life that is morally just. Seek the truth always. Be respectful and respectable. Proudly wear the robe of righteousness that I have given you. Glorify me, and you will be filled with my Spirit.

Blessed are you when your heart is pure and innocent. You will see me. Keep your heart from being adulterated. Do not let the world contaminate your passions. Do not allow your thinking to be polluted with obscenities and immorality. Do not mingle with those who are slanted toward evil. Remain chaste and uncorrupted in your behavior. Set your eyes on the things above rather than the things of this world. Put blinders on your eyes, and keep your focus on me. Glorify me with your life. Live a clean life; and you will catch glimpses of me.

When you go against the patterns of the world, you may be mistreated. When you live a pure and blameless life, people may insult you because of me. Others may speak evil of you when your life becomes a witness of my goodness. You may be hated and excluded because you belong to me. I tell you, rejoice in your suffering. Blessed are you when you are persecuted because of righteousness. Your compensation in heaven will be remarkable. Celebrate when you are discriminated against because of the testimony you are to me. I hold a distinguished place in heaven for you. Great is your eternal reward when you glorify me.

Glorify the Lord with me; let us exalt his name together. (Psalm 34:3)

Glorify the Lord with Me

Lord, be glorified in me. I will exalt your name, and lift your name on high. Lord, receive the glory I give you. I proclaim your greatness to all the earth. You have delivered me from my suffering. You exchanged my heavy load for a lighter one. I do not bear my burdens alone, but you are with me always. You lend your ear to my cries. You hear me call for your help. You do not travel far to find me. You know my exact location, because you never leave my side. You are with me always. I will lean on you when I am weak and weary. I will find my strength in you. Glorify the Lord with me.

Lord, you have protected me and prospered me. I owe you my life. You saved me from my sin and lawlessness. You helped me turn from my wicked ways. You have set up residence in my heart. The living God lives in me. Be glorified in me as I lift my praises to you. My spirit joins with your Spirit in praise of your holy name. You are faithful to all ages and generations. You do not neglect me as undeserving as I am. You grace me with your presence. Lord, I humbly bow before you, and exalt you on your throne. Glorify the Lord with me.

I do not fear the end of my days because I belong to you. My future in heaven is secure because I believe in you. Eternity is within my grasp because of your saving grace. Thank you for the sacrifice you made when you gave your Son's life in exchange for mine. You took away all the punishment I deserved, and clothed me in your robe of righteousness. You call me your own, an heir of your eternal wealth. Glorify the Lord with me.

I lift up my hands unto the heavens and glorify your name. I sing praises to your holy name. You are great and worthy of my praise. You are the mighty one, the ruler of all the earth. Yet you call me your child, a child of the King. Glory to God! Glorify the Lord with me.

Praise the Lord, O my soul. (Psalm 104:1a)

Lord, Hear My Praise

Lord, you are mighty and mysterious. You're my strength for each new day.
You are the bright Morning Star that leads me on my way.
My Father and forgiver, my comfort and my guide,
You love me more than anything. For me your Son has died.
You protect me from my enemy. You guard me with your shield.
Your Word, a sword in my hand, to my foe, I will not yield.
Lord, I lift your name above the earth. I exalt you on your throne.
There is no other like you. I will worship you alone.
Praise you King of glory, the Son of God Most High.
Praise the Lord, O my soul, for me you came to die.
Thank you for your priceless gift—God's Spirit you did send.
He dwells deep within my heart and is my closest friend.

The Lord is a refuge for the oppressed, a stronghold in times of trouble. (Psalm 9:9)

My Refuge and My Rock

Lord, you are my shelter when I am broken. I owe my life to you. In times of difficulty, I cling to you. When my way seems uncertain, you are my guide. When I am weak and weary from my journey, you are the rock I rest against. Lord, hold me in your arms today, even carry me. Please lighten the load I bring. My burden is much too heavy; it's more than I can endure.

I look unto the heavens; my soul longs for you. I thirst for you as I wander through the desert. I am surrounded by emptiness, but you comfort me. I feel lost and lonely, but you are here. I call out your name, and you answer me.

You are my refuge and my stronghold. I find my rest in you. You lift me out of the pit I am in. You renew my strength, and set my feet on solid ground. You are my foundation. I will not fall to such depths again. You are my guard. You keep my foot from stumbling. You clear the path ahead of me. You lead me into righteousness for the sake of your name.

You protect me from evil. You are my defender. You place your armor upon my bruised and tired body. You are my helmet and my shield. No arrows shall pierce my mind or my heart. No deceit will I hold on to. You replace the lies of my enemy, with your good and perfect truth. You shed light into the darkness. You expose the enemy's ways. I will not be defeated. You are on my side.

I praise you, O Lord, with all of my soul. My lips sing praise to your name. My heart is devoted to you, Most Holy One. You are my mighty refuge, my stronghold in times of trouble. I owe you my full devotion. I give myself to you. Your name is awesome and majestic. I give glory to your name. You deserve all glory, honor, and praise. Blessed be your name, O Lord. Blessed be your name.

"I am the Alpha and the Omega, the First and the Last, the Beginning and the End." (Revelation 22:13)

Three in One

Lord, you are high and lifted up. You are seated on the throne of glory. I give praise to your holy name. Let all the earth rejoice. My praise is worthy of you alone. You are the Most High God. You are the King of kings—the Lord of lords. I boast that I am known by you. You designed me, and created me to love you and worship you. Let me fulfill my purpose, Lord, and praise you admirably. I exalt you above everything. I worship you with my whole heart, mind, and soul. With every ounce of strength you have given me, I proclaim you as my Lord.

Father, I adore you. You are my protector and provider. You keep me safe from harm, and lavish me with your love. You give me all I need. No one else can satisfy my desires. No one on this earth will ever love me perfectly; but you, Father, you know what I need before I ask. You hem me in behind me and before me, and let no evil thing overtake me. Nothing happens to me without your knowledge and approval. You allow me opportunities to grow, but you never leave my side. You are with me always. I respect you, and I love you, Father.

Jesus, I admire you. You left your throne in heaven to be with me. You walked the earth, and now you walk with me. You call me your friend. You teach me everything I need to know. You show me how to love perfectly. You sacrificed yourself for me. You died in my place. You victoriously conquered death. You defeated my enemy. I am triumphant over death because of you. You have paid my ransom. I will live forever in the house of the Lord. I owe everything I have to you. You are my Savior and my Lord. I worship you with all I am.

Spirit, I honor you. You have taken up residence in my being. You comfort me and guide me. You remind me of everything Jesus taught. You are my Counselor. You speak truth into my life. You expose the darkness, and overpower it with light. You guide me into all truth. You speak to me as a friend. You encourage me. You cover me with your love. You grant me wisdom and knowledge. You affirm me and give me hope. You are gentle, but firm. You are powerful and just. You are God in me.

Father, Son, and Holy Spirit, you are the great triune God. I bow down and worship you. You are the Alpha and Omega; the Beginning and the End. You are my all in all. In you alone, I will put my trust. You have my devotion; all I have to give you. I worship you in power and in might. You alone deserve my worship. You alone deserve my praise. I give thanks to you for all you have done. I adore you. I acclaim you. I exalt you. I give you my praise.

May my lips overflow with praise, for you teach me your decrees. May my tongue sing of your word, for all your commands are righteous. (Psalm 119:171-172)

My Lips Overflow with Praise

O Lord, I lift up my praise unto your holy name. Unto the heavens, I lift up my hands to glorify you. You, my Lord, are seated on the throne of heaven. You hear my praises; they bring warmth to your heart. I am humbled in your presence. I fall to my knees; even prostrate, I lie before you. I glorify you with thanksgiving. I am blessed to be called your child.

My praises resound in the heavens. A choir of heavenly hosts accompanies me, "Hosanna in the highest—Hosanna is your name—Savior of all the earth—Hosanna we proclaim." Your power and might are limitless. I am exhausted in your presence. I am blinded by the light that radiates from you. I exalt you above the earth; you are the King of heaven.

I sing aloud a new song. Your Word is on my lips. Your ways are just and holy. You are the righteous judge of all men. I am unworthy to be in your presence. I count my blessings before you. With thanksgiving, I pour out my heart to you. I raise my voice to your ears. Hear, O Lord, my songs to you. Let them be a fragrant offering to you.

Your dominion over all the earth radiates from your throne. With authority you rule your kingdom on earth, as it is in heaven. You are majestic in power and might. Your enemies bow down before you. Even the rocks cry out in praise of your holiness. A song of devotion spills forth from my mouth. My lips overflow with praises to you.

Heal me, O Lord, and I will be healed; save me and I will be saved, for you are the one I praise. (Jeremiah 17:14)

You are the One I Praise

I praise you, O Lord, because you have saved me. You saved me from a life of sin. I am forgiven because you paid the penalty for my sin. You saved me from my self-destructive ways. You gave me a reason to live. You took my sin upon yourself, and made me righteous by your grace. Lord, you are great and worthy of my praise. You are the most excellent, amazing God. You love me when I am unlovable. You call me your child. I will glorify your name alone.

I praise you, O Lord, because you have healed me. When my heart was heavy, and I was despondent, you took my burdens upon yourself, and gave me a lighter load. You reached down into the pit, and pulled me up with your own hands. You saved me from the depths of darkness that held me its prisoner, and you lifted me into the light of a new day. I was shattered into a thousand pieces, and you restored my body, mind, and soul. You comforted me and rebuilt me on top of your firm foundation. I am alive and well because of your great mercy. O Lord, I give you all of my praise. The glory belongs to you alone. You are great and worthy of all my praise.

I praise you, O Lord, because you have given me a life of peace. You turned my crazy life around. You took the chaos and put it into order. You gave me hope, and set me on the path you had laid out for me. Your ways are much higher than my ways, Lord. You know where I belong. The life you have designed for me is far greater than anything I could ever ask or imagine. You saved me from the path of destruction. You pulled me from the battle, and clothed me with your peace. I did not escape the fight unscathed, but you have healed my wounds. You saw my brokenness, and lovingly, glued me back together. You are great and worthy of all my praise. I will lift up your name in honor and admiration. You are my healer and my Savior. I raise my voice with shouts of acclamation. I give you thanks for all you have done for me.

One generation will commend your works to another; they will tell of your mighty acts. They will speak of the glorious splendor of your majesty, and I will meditate on your wonderful works. They will tell of the power of your awesome works, and I will proclaim your great deeds. They will celebrate your abundant goodness and joyfully sing of your righteousness. (Psalm 145:4-7)

The Splendor of Your Majesty

Lord, you are great and worthy of my praise. I will praise your name and commend your works to my children. I will tell my children's children of your mighty acts. One generation will stand with the next, and we will raise our voices in honor and praise of your name. We will share the splendor of your magnificence with generations to come.

I meditate on your amazing handiwork. I will convey the majesty of all your creation. Your deeds are fantastic and worthy of our praise. We will celebrate your loving kindness, and sing wholeheartedly of your justice. You are the Lord most righteous. You deal honestly and fairly in the judgments you impart. You are gracious with your mercy, even when we are so undeserving. Compassion flows from your heart, and forgiveness you hold in your hand. You are abounding in love and good to all. All you have made will glorify your name.

We will tell of your holiness, and articulate your strength. The whole world will know of your mighty power and the splendor of your everlasting kingdom. We will teach our children of your faithfulness. You are true to your promises. You satisfy the desires of those who delight in you. You are near to all who call on you. You hear our cries, and save us from all our unrighteousness.

Let all your creation praise your holy name. You meet the needs of every living thing you created. We all look to you, and lift our praises to you in your heavenly realm. You are the King of all creation. You reign over all the earth. Your kingdom is glorious. From one generation to the next, we will praise you as long as we live. We will sing and dance before your throne. We will proclaim the splendor of your majesty. O God, forever you will reign.

Let everything that has breath praise the Lord. Praise the Lord. (Psalm 150:6)

Let Us Praise the Lord

Let us praise the Lord of all the earth. Let us praise him on his throne.
Let us praise God in the heights of heaven. Let us praise his name alone.
Let us praise the Father, God our King. We lift our voice in song.
Let us praise him with a thousand tongues. We praise him in the throng.
Let everything that draws a breath, sing praises to the Lord.
Let every creature, fish, and bird burst out in one accord.
Let every man, woman, boy, and girl lift up his holy name.
Let the young and old, rich and poor, proudly do the same.
Let us praise the King of glory as he sits in heaven on high.
Let us praise the bright Morning Star that shines up in the sky.
Let us praise the man of sorrows, who died in our place.
Let us praise the Son of God, who saved us by his grace.
Let every nation, tribe, and tongue give glory to the Lamb.
Let the rocks cry out in holy praise unto the great I AM.
Let everything that draws a breath, sing praise in one accord.
Let all the angel choirs sing their praises to the Lord.
Let us bow before Almighty God with his Son at his right hand.
Let the praises ring out loud and clear from every corner of every land.
Let everything that has a breath, praise the Lord of heaven and earth.
Let us lift our voices to our Lord in praise of his great worth.
Let everything that has breath praise the Lord. Praise the Lord!

Then I heard every creature in heaven and on earth and under the earth and on the sea, and all that is in them, singing: "To him who sits on the throne and to the Lamb be praise and honor and glory and power, for ever and ever!" (Revelation 5:13)

Worthy is the Lamb

Lord, you are worthy of all praise and honor and glory and power forever! I can't wait to join with the angel choirs in singing their praises to you, as you sit on your throne in heaven. When that day comes, every knee will bow down, and worship the Lamb who sits at the right hand of God. You deserve all our praise. Every creature in every corner of the earth, sky, and sea will sing: "Worthy is the Lamb!"

Lord, I feel so unworthy compared to your greatness. I am so incompetent to give you all the glory you deserve. My worship of you pales in comparison to the enormity of praise you merit. I am not worthy to approach your throne. I fall to my knees and praise your name. I lie down on the ground face first because I am not worthy even to kneel before you. I will sing and dance before you in your honor. I will praise you forever in song.

Lord, I am anxious for the day when I will see you face to face. All the light of a thousand sunsets will shine brilliantly from your face. You will remove the blindness from my eyes, and give me new eyes to see you in all your glory. I will not be blinded by your light this time, because the eyes you will give me are designed by you to reflect the light of your glory back to yourself.

You will loosen my tongue, and give me a new tongue to praise you with. I will sing of your great redeeming praise with a thousand other tongues. You will clothe me in my wedding attire, because my bridegroom awaits my entrance to the wedding feast. I assemble myself in the gathering of the bride, your church, as the wife of the Lamb of God. All the wedding guests will sing in unison: "Worthy is the Lamb of God of all praise and honor and glory and power, forever and ever!"

If anyone speaks, he should do it as one speaking the very words of God. If anyone serves, he should do it with the strength God provides, so that in all things God may be praised through Jesus Christ. To him be the glory and the power for ever and ever. Amen. (1 Peter 4:11)

To God Be the Glory

Lord, let my life be a sweet offering of praise to your holy name. I pray that my words and my actions would bring glory to you alone. If I should speak, allow me to speak only the words that you provide me. If it is time to hold my tongue, let me be diligent in my restraint. Lord, let the language that flows from my mouth always be respectful to my God and King. Let every term I use to express myself be considerate of your excellent principles. I lift up my speech before you, and ask for your blessing in everything I say.

Lord, teach me to serve others as you have served. Provide me with your strength to work diligently, as I wait on or assist another. Let me be humble in my service, always considering others greater than myself. Let me lay down my own desires to put your requests before my own. Lord, I want to serve others, as if I were serving you. May you be praised through Jesus Christ, as I serve the way you have trained me.

Lord, I take no credit for my words or my service. I live a borrowed life from you. It is my hope that I will bring the greatest glory to you. You deserve all the credit for anything accomplished through me. It is by your strength and power alone that the assignments you give me are ever completed. Let your work through your servant be blessed to be a blessing to those who receive it. It is with every ounce of fortitude I have that I lift up your name to the heavens. My adoration of you is so insignificant compared to your greatness and your power. Let my offering of worship provide you with a sweet aroma of praise as you receive it. I lift my hands and voice in honor of your name. You alone are worthy of my praise. To God be the glory!

O Lord, open my lips, and my mouth will declare your praise. You do not delight in sacrifice, or I would bring it; you do not take pleasure in burnt offerings. The sacrifices of God are a broken spirit; a broken and contrite heart, O God, you will not despise. (Psalm 51:15-17)

My Sacrifice to You, O God

O Lord, I open my lips and my mouth declares your praise. You are an awesome God. Your mercy is given to me in generous portions; portions I do not deserve. Your compassions never fail me. Your forgiveness does not cease. You are sympathetic to my human state. When I fall down, you help me up. When I stumble, you clear a path for me. When I kneel down, you hear my cries. I am not worthy to present myself to you, but you welcome me with open arms.

O Lord, you do not delight in sacrifice or that is what I would bring. You do not take pleasure in burnt offerings or that is the process I would follow. You have already made the provision for me. You sent your one and only Son, as the sacrificial Lamb, to pay the debt for my sin. I am forever indebted to you, but you say it is not so. In your eyes, my obligation has been satisfied. Your plan is perfect, but I am not. I accepted your work on the cross, and yet I continue to sin against you. O Lord, how many more times will you forgive me?

O God, my Father, will you forgive me once more? I come before you humbly, on both knees, and beg you for your mercy. Will you pardon my unrighteous acts? My sacrifice to you, O God, is my broken and contrite heart. I regret my poor decisions. I am ashamed of my lack of self-control. I apologize when I have turned my face from you. I am sorry for my sins. Will you accept the offering I give you once again— my heart? Your atoning work on the cross has already compensated for my trespasses; but I must repent, and ask for your clemency again. Wash me, and I will be whiter than snow. Cleanse my heart within me, and renew a right spirit in me. Do not despise me, but accept my gift of sacrifice to you—my broken and contrite heart. Your mercy is unending. Your love for me is immense. Restore in my heart the joy of your salvation. My newly restored heart belongs to you; I place it at your feet.

Give thanks to the Lord, call on his name; make known among the nations what he has done. Sing to him, sing praise to him; tell of all his wonderful acts. Glory in his holy name; let the hearts of those who seek the Lord rejoice. Look to the Lord and his strength; seek his face always. (1 Chronicles 16:8-11)

Glory in His Holy Name

Lord, I give thanks to you because of your goodness. Your love goes on forever. I call on you in the middle of the night because you never sleep. I beckon you all day long because you are always at my side. Day and night, I sing my praises to you. You are available to me anytime I need you. You rescue me from myself. You save me from my sin. You protect me from my enemies. You deliver me from evil. You give me food and drink. I find my rest in you. You are the shepherd who watches over me. You draw me close with your staff. You discipline me with your rod of correction. You carry me in your arms. You shelter me from the storm. You lavish me with your love and grace. How is it that you would call me your child?

I will rejoice in you always, as I seek your face for all of eternity. Your presence is made known to me. You give me your Spirit, and teach me your ways. I will find my refuge in you. I look to you for my strength. I will glorify you in the sanctuary. I will praise you in the streets. I will tell of your mighty deeds, the wonders of your grace and mercy. The greatness of your love is difficult to impart, but I will do my best to proclaim you and your wonderful acts. Your love is like a mighty mountain—strong and unchanging. Nothing but my own sin will separate me from you. No sin is too big for you to forgive. No request is too small for me to ask of you.

I will praise you in the morning. At noon, I will glorify your name. In the hours of the evening, I will remember you. All day long my lips will sing you songs of praise. All day long my heart is devoted to you. I will recount your goodness and your powerful deeds. I will proclaim your grandeur and your abounding love. I am blessed with the peace you give me, which surpasses my comprehension. I give you all my praise and I glorify your holy name.

When he was gone, Jesus said, "Now is the Son of Man glorified and God is glorified in him. If God is glorified in him, God will glorify the Son in himself, and will glorify him at once." (John 13:31-32)

God is Glorified in Him

O God, I exalt your name. I praise you, Father, Son, and Holy Spirit. God, my Father, you are glorified in the work of your Son, Jesus Christ, who was glorified in the gift of his self-sacrifice. Jesus, my Lord, willingly, obediently carried out your will with his death on the cross. He bridged the chasm between you and me, and provided my way to reconciliation with you. Your plan of salvation was made possible by your one and only Son. God, you are glorified in him. You have exalted your Son. He is seated at your right hand. You have given him authority over everything on the earth, in the heavens above, and under the earth.

Father, Son, and Holy Spirit, I pay tribute to you. I applaud your works, the wonders you perform. The Father gave the Son, the Son gave the Holy Spirit, and all were given for my sake. I owe you all the glory, honor, and praise you are due. My hands will not hang limp as I praise you. I lift up your name in holy worship. You are seated on the throne of glory, above the heavens. You deserve my heart's allegiance and my life's devotion. I give you my heart and my life. Would you be glorified in me, O Lord, my God?

You are the Most High God, and you call me your child. I live in the righteousness you provide. I will bless your name, my Abba. You are my life's purpose. All that I do, I do for you. You deserve much more glory than I am capable of giving you. I do my best to praise you and it does not seem nearly enough. My mind is short on words to describe you. I cannot take in the full magnitude of your grace. I am not worthy to be called your child. You gave your life for a disgrace like me. Now I give my life to you. Transform me into your likeness. Be glorified in the work of your Son. Be glorified in me because of his work. I give you my heart full of praise.

I have seen you in the sanctuary and beheld your power and your glory. Because your love is better than life, my lips will glorify you. I will praise you as long as I live, and in your name I will lift up my hands. (Psalm 63:2-4)

Your Love is Better than Life

O Lord, I will praise you as long as I live. I lift up my hands in praise of your holy name. I take refuge in the sanctuary you provide for me. You have given me a shelter, a safe haven to rest. I have seen your hand on my life. I have seen your power in the amazing work of your hands. Your miracles and spectacular deeds speak for themselves in honor of you. Your righteousness shines like the brightest sun in the mid-day sky, like the most vivid star at night.

I have considered your magnificent splendor. You are more brilliant than my eyes can tolerate. I turn my face from your radiance. I fall to the ground in worship of you. Accept my humble adoration. You are the Most High God. Your name is lifted up above all kings of the earth and all lords of the land. You are the King of all kings and the Lord of all lords. You reign on earth and in the heavenly realms. Your kingdoms bow down to you in reverence and devotion. The heavens declare your glorious splendor. Receive all the praise you are due.

My lips will glorify you because of your great love. Your love is better than life. You created my inmost being. You formed me in my mother's womb. You know me better than anyone, and you love me just the same. I am alive and well because of your wonderful love. You love me more than I love myself. You love me no matter the cost. You paid the ransom for my soul. I am forever in your debt with my gratitude. You fought for my heart and won the battle. You are my shining knight, the keeper of my heart. You protect me in your arms of love, and give me your righteousness. I give you all the thanks my mouth can gather. I will lift up my hands in praise of you as long as I live. Your love is greater than anything else I can imagine. Your love reaches outside the capacity of my mind. Your love is better than life.

"Yet a time is coming and has now come when the true worshipers will worship the Father in spirit and truth, for they are the kind of worshipers the Father seeks. God is spirit, and his worshipers must worship in spirit and truth." (John 4:23-24)

In Spirit and in Truth

Father God in heaven, I want to be the kind of true worshiper that is pleasing to you. Teach me your ways. Let your Spirit reign in my heart. Allow my spirit to join with the Holy Spirit in praise of your majestic name. My praise alone is not worthy of your greatness; but united with the Spirit you have given me, I pray that my worship would send the sweet aroma of authentic admiration to the heavens for you to enjoy. I lift my praise to you with every ounce of strength in my body. I am determined to exalt you above everything else, and hold you in the highest place of honor. You are worthy of my wholehearted worship. I offer you my heart as my sacrifice to you. Would you be pleased to accept my humble adoration today?

God, you search the earth for genuine spirits who are dedicated to living a life of righteousness, and who would worship you in power and strength. I am not worthy to place my worship at your feet, but please accept the praise and devotion I give you. It is all that I have to offer you. I will worship you in the power and strength of the Holy Spirit you sent me. Your Spirit teaches my spirit to exalt you enthusiastically with zeal and fervor. Thank you for providing me with opportunities to give you all the honor, glory, and praise you deserve.

O Lord, my Maker, you designed me to worship you. Let me fulfill your purpose, and give you glory, honor, and praise all the days of my life here on earth and in the life to come. I will worship you with all of my heart, soul, mind, and strength. My body trembles with the rush of pleasing you with my reverence. All of the love you have given me is channeled back to you, as I lift my voice in adulation. I am not capable of blessing you the way you have blessed me. I pray my faithful devotion and passionate enthusiasm brings you the highest honor and glory.

"You are worthy, our Lord and God, to receive glory and honor and power, for you created all things, and by your will they were created and have their being." *(Revelation 4:11)*

You are Worthy

O Lord, my Creator, you created all things by your will. You created the heavens and the earth. You created light, and separated it from darkness. You divided the waters into the sea and the sky. The dry ground appeared at the instruction of your will. You produced plants and trees of all kinds. You hung the sun, moon, and stars in the sky, and set the planets into orbit. You spoke into existence the fish of the sea and the birds of the air. You commanded the land to produce animals. In your image, you created man and woman. You saw all that you made, and it was very good. You are worthy to receive all glory, honor, and praise.

O Lord, my Creator, you created me, and called me your child. You formed me with your own hands, and placed me in my mother's womb. In awe and wonder, you synchronized my tiny heart with yours, and established my first breath. Before I speak a word, you know what I will say. You know my thoughts before my mind forms them. You fill my heart with your Spirit. You transform my life by your amazing power. You protect me from evil, and set me on the right path. You created me, and I am good. You are worthy to receive all glory, honor, and praise.

O Lord, my Creator, you created a plan of salvation so that I could be reconciled to you. I was trapped in my sin. I had nowhere to turn. I could not run any farther away from you, but you did not lose sight of me. You hemmed me in, before me and behind me. You supported me when I could not stand. You carried me when I could not walk. You removed my heavy load, and traded it for a lighter one. You removed my yoke of slavery, and now I am yoked with you. You paid the penalty for my sin. You died on the cross and set me free. I have given you my heart. You are my Savior and my Lord. You have given me a new life, and it is good—a life everlasting, and it is very, very good. You are worthy to receive all glory, honor, and praise.

For the Lord is good and his love endures forever; his faithfulness continues through all generations. (Psalm 100:5)

God is Good

You are the Lord of all creation, and you are good! I praise you with shouts of joy. You are Lord over all the earth. I come before you in joyful song, and serve you with the gladness of my heart. I know that you are God, and you are very good. Your love is unconditional, and it does not end. You created me. I am not my own work. I belong to you—a sheep in your fold.

I will enter into your presence with thanksgiving. I bring to you my heartfelt praise. I am thankful for your goodness. Your faithfulness goes on and on. Your love lasts forever. I give you the honor you deserve. I proclaim you in your righteousness. I worship you in your splendor. I declare your glory before all men. All power, strength, and majesty belong to you.

The heavens rejoice in your name. The rocks cry out with their worship. The whole earth trembles before you. We exalt thee, O God. Your kindness, goodness, and mercy have been true through all generations. You are a loving, forgiving God who washes away my sin. I am unworthy to approach your throne, but you take up your residence in me. I have no value without you. I am nothing on my own.

I kneel before you, my Maker. I bow down in worship of you. You are the King of kings and Lord of lords, the most excellent high priest. You are the rock of my salvation. My foundation is sure in you. I proclaim your love in the presence of many witnesses. Your goodness is worthy of my tribute. Let the whole earth sing you praises, and tell about the wonders of your love. You are the Most High God who lives and reigns in the heavens and the earth. You are above all things. Glorious is your name. Receive all my honor and praise. I cannot keep my tongue silent in your presence. Let the whole earth extol you. May everything that draws a breath, praise your name!

Remember your word to your servant, for you have given me hope. My comfort in my suffering is this: Your promise renews my life. (Psalm 119:49-50)

My Comforter

O Lord, you have been my comfort in times of loss. You have carried me through times of great difficulty. You have carried me through the loss of my loved ones. You have carried me through the darkness of depression. You have walked with me through the shadows of gloom to the light on the other side. You have turned my life from upside down to right side up.

O Lord, my Comforter, you have comforted me with great compassion and understanding. You weep when I weep; you mourn when I mourn. Blessed be the name of the Lord who comforts his people in their deep sadness. In the midst of my mourning, you give me hope, and renew my life with your promise. You are my strength when I am weak. You assist me when I cannot put one foot in front of the other. You show me the way. You light my path, and extend your hand to me. The assurance of your promises inspires me to go on.

You lift me up out of the pit I am in, and place my feet on solid ground. You remove my sackcloth, and clothe me with joy. Your name is great and worthy of my praise. I sing a new song, because of your love. I look forward to a new life in you. You restore my soul and faith in you. I anticipate the days ahead with great optimism. You encourage me on my journey. The road is long, but you are my portion. The way is not smooth, but you are my guide.

There will be trouble along the way, but you are my refuge. I call your name, and you answer me. When my foot slips, you catch me before I fall. You are my bridge across the deep gorge. I am uncertain of my way, but you give me the confidence that you are in control. You carry my burden, and give me a lighter load to bear. I will go on, because I am yoked with you. You teach me to persevere. I press on with my focus on you.

You are the light for my path, my rock and my refuge, my strength and my guide. Blessed be your name, O Lord. I survive my trials because of your great love for me. I am alive in you, because you live in me. Great are you, Lord, and worthy of praise. You are my Comforter.

"The Lord is my strength and my song; he has become my salvation. He is my God, and I will praise him, my father's God, and I will exalt him. The Lord is a warrior; the Lord is his name." (Exodus 15:2-3)

The Lord is a Warrior

O Lord, you are my God, and I will praise you forever. You are the new song I have in my heart—the song that I sing of, the breath I breathe in. You give life to my body and strength to my spirit. I will exalt you on your throne. You are my light and my salvation. I will fear nothing because you are with me. My enemy pursues me, but you, O God, stand with me, my defender and my protector. He has met his match with you. You simply open your mouth and destroy my opponent. Your majestic right hand throws him down in an instant. You say the word, and he falls to his destruction. The Lord is a warrior; the Lord is his name. Your majestic power speaks of itself.

No other god is like you. You are righteous and holy, set apart from all others. You are awesome in glory, your brilliance is blinding. You are wonderful in your works; I know that first hand. Your love is unfailing. Your mercy is immense. You are my salvation, my warrior God. You wipe out my adversary with one strike of your mighty hand. You are the Most High God. You are El Shaddai—my strength and my shield. You deliver me from the hands of my foe.

You lead me out of the battle to your holy dwelling place, the place you have prepared for the redeemed. You plant me on the mountain of your inheritance, where I will spend my eternity with you. You resume your place on your throne. You will reign forever and ever. You rule over all the earth and everything in it. You control the heavens and the seas. You oversee your creation day and night. You never sleep or slumber. You are always with me. I am your child, and you are my King. I am your friend, and you are my God. I am your bride, and you are my husband. You fight in my defense, time after time. You are my righteous, majestic warrior.

MY PRAYER FOR SALVATION

*I accept the free gift of God's grace
and claim my salvation in Christ.*

That if you confess with your mouth, "Jesus is Lord," and believe in your heart that God raised him from the dead, you will be saved. For it is with your heart that you believe and are justified, and it is with your mouth that you confess and are saved. (Romans 10:9-10)

My Prayer for Salvation

"My Father God, I confess that I am a sinner. My sins have separated me from you. I ask for your forgiveness. Please cleanse me from all unrighteousness. I desire to live a life that is pleasing to you. I believe in my heart that your Son, Jesus Christ, died for my sins. I believe that you raised him from the dead, and seated him on the throne at your right hand. I confess with my mouth, 'Jesus is Lord.' Please save me from my sins, and transform me into your likeness. Thank you for your amazing gift of saving grace. Thank you for the gift of your Holy Spirit who you send, in this moment, to live in my heart. I want to live a Spirit-filled life. Allow me to hear your voice in my thoughts. I desire an intimate relationship with you. In the precious name of Jesus, my Savior and Lord, I pray. Amen."

. . . .

If you have said this prayer of confession, and believe it in your heart, God's Word in Scripture promises that you will be saved from your sins, and receive the gift of eternal life. Congratulations, and welcome to the family of believers! This calls for a celebration! Allow the Holy Spirit to transform your life, and sanctify you through and through, as you become more like Jesus every day. You are a child of the King, and you will recognize God's voice. Seek God daily by finding a place away from the crowds and the noise, and listening to the voice of the Holy Spirit who lives inside you. The God of the universe desires to be in intimate relationship with each of his children. Speak with God daily, and discover who he is by reading the Scripture, and listening to his voice. Once you listen and hear God's voice, you will never be the same again.

If you have just received the gift of God's grace, and accepted Jesus Christ as your Savior, please send me an email telling me so. I would love to pray for you, and help you get started in your journey of knowing and following the Lord. You may email me at: sindynagel612@aol.com.

Blessings in Christ,

Sindy